The Sharing Circle Handbook

Topics for Teaching Self-Awareness, Communication, and Social Skills

Susanna Palomares
Sandy Schuster
Cheryl Watkins

INNERCHOICE PUBLISHING

Editor: Dianne Schilling

ISBN 1-56499-007-9

INNERCHOICE PUBLISHING
P.O. Box 1185, Torrance, CA 90505
(310) 816-3085, (800) 662-9662
Fax: (310) 816-3092
E-Mail: blwjalmar@worldnet.att.net

Dedication

This book is dedicated to Dr. Gerry Dunne, who's pioneering work, beginning in the mid 1960s, has shaped and directed the entire affective education movement. Dr. Dunne, through her co-authorship of the Magic Circle Program, developed the first curriculum materials utilizing the unique circle discussion process. Long before anything resembling this process existed in schools, Dr. Dunne recognized the need to address the social and emotional development of children through activities that teachers and counselors would find compatible with their existing skills and, therefore, easy to implement. Her convictions, commitment, and extraordinary efforts on behalf of the well-being of children have been our inspiration and, indeed, have made this book possible.

Contents

This section discusses the theory underlying the Sharing Circle process. The targeted growth areas of Communication, Self-Awareness, Personal Mastery, and Interpersonal Skills are covered in some detail.

To make implementation easy, many of the most frequently asked questions about organizing and beginning Sharing Circles are answered, and ideas to help facilitate immediate use are provided.

This section is a thorough guide to conducting Sharing Circles. It covers major points to keep in mind and answers questions which will arise as you begin the program.

Sharing Circles provide a natural setting for students to develop leadership skills. This section contains everything you'll need to make the transition from adult-led to student-led circles.

Many teachers and counselors have occasion to create sharing circles tailored to a particular subject, lesson, or student need. This section offers guidelines and suggestions to facilitate that process.

Here is a collection of answers to the most frequently asked questions about Sharing Circles. Answers are grouped to address the leader's role, classroom management, student responses, and process and content areas.

For leaders who have mastered the basics, this list of suggestions offers additional insights into the Sharing Circle process and the leader's role within that process.

Sharing Circle Topics

My Favorite Vacation
A Secret Wish I Have
What I Would Do If I Inherited One Million Dollars

A Place Where I Feel Serene and at Peace
Someone I Would Like to Know Better
What I Think the World Needs To Be a Better Place
The Craziest Dream I Ever Had
I Did Something Dreaming That I Couldn't Do Awake
A Name I'd Like to Have
A Special Occasion or Holiday Related to My Culture That
    I Appreciate
One Of My Favorite Possessions
The Funniest Thing That Ever Happened To Me
My All-Time Favorite Movie
A Person I'd Like To Be Like
My Idea of a Perfect Saturday Afternoon
The Best News I Could Get Right Now
One of the Best Things That Ever Happened to Me
If I Had One Wish, It Would Be...
What I Would Do If I Were Made King or Queen of the World
    for One Day

The Worst Trouble I Ever Got Into
One Way I Wish I Could be Different
A Secret Fear I Have
A Significant Event in My Life
Something I Want to Keep
One Question I Have About Life
My Greatest Asset
Something I Need Help With
Something About Me You Wouldn't Know Unless I Told You
A Talent That I Possess
Something I Like to Do Alone
Two Things I Believe In That Conflict with Each Other
A Time I Stood Up for Something I Strongly Believe In
Part of Me Wanted to Do One Thing, and Part of Me Wanted
    to Do Another
I Said Yes When I Wanted to Say No
I Perceived Something Because It Was What I Wanted to
    Perceive
An Experience I Had That Caused Me to See Things
    Differently
When I Felt Comfortable Just Being Me
Something I Hate To Do
Something I Like About Myself Right Now
One Thing I Am Sure I Can Do Well
I Did Something That Made Me Feel Like a Good Person
Why I Sometimes Like To Be Alone

I Felt Good Enough About Myself to Reach Out to
    Someone Else
After I Got to Know Someone, I Liked Him or Her,
    Even Though I Didn't At First
Someone Who Trusts Me

The School Rule I Think Is Most Important
I Do My Best in School When . . .
How I Feel About Homework
What I Like Most About This School
A Change I Would Make to Improve This School
How I Learn Best

What I Think Good Communication Is
Someone Pointed Out Something Good About Me
When What Was Said Was Not What Was Meant
A Time When I Accepted Someone Else's Feelings
A Time When It Was Okay to Express My Feelings
Once When Someone Wouldn't Listen to Me
How I Get People to Pay Attention to Me
A Time When Listening Would Have Kept Me Out Of
    Trouble
I Told Someone How I Was Feeling
A Time I Listened Well to Someone
Something I See Differently Than My Parents' Generation
    Sees It
How I Used Sharing Circle Skills Outside the Circle

What I Would Do if I Were an Adult
Something Worth Saving For
A Success I Recently Experienced
Something I Would Like To Achieve in the Next Three Years
Something I Wish I Could Do Better
Something I Want
When I Got to Share in Making a Decision
Something I Want, But Am Afraid to Ask For
A Time I Won and Loved It
A Time I Lost and Took It Hard
First I Imagined It, and Then I Created It
When Someone Expected the Very Best of Me
Things I Can Do To Get Where I Want To Be
What I Could Do To Be a Good Parent
How I Earned Something and What I Did With It
I Had a Problem and Solved It

Introduction

This collection of Sharing Circles has been designed for implementation using the Sharing Circle process (rules and leadership procedures) described in this book. If you have not had prior experience with Sharing Circles, we recommend that you read pages 11 to 22 before attempting to lead your first circle.

In particular, we urge you to respect the integrity of the sharing and discussion phases of the circle. These two phases are procedurally and qualitatively different, yet of equal importance in promoting awareness, insight, and higher-level thinking in students. The longer you lead Sharing Circles, the more you will appreciate the instructional advantages of maintaining this unique relationship.

All of the topics are intended to develop awareness and insight through voluntary sharing. The discussion questions allow students to understand what has been shared at deeper levels, to evaluate ideas that have been generated by the topic, and to apply specific concepts to other areas of learning. If you wish to make connections between the topics and your regular curriculum, you can accomplish this by adding discussion questions designed to achieve that end.

The topic elaborations provided under the heading, "Introducing the Topic" are given as a guide and do not necessarily have to be presented verbatim. Once you have used Sharing Circles for awhile and are feeling comfortable with the process, you will most assuredly want to substitute your own words of introduction. We are merely providing you with ideas.

In your elaboration, try to use language and examples that are appropriate to the age, ability, and culture of your students. In our suggested examples we have tried to be as general as possible; however, those examples may not be the most appropriate for your students.

Through this book, you and your students are about to embark on a wondrous journey of growth and discovery. We are confident that the Sharing Circle will enrich the learning experiences you create in your classroom, just as it has for so many other teachers and students around the country. Enjoy!

An Overview of Sharing Circles

In order for students to lead fulfilling, productive lives, they first need to experience the fullness of themselves. They need to know who they are, how they function, and how they relate to others. They also need to believe in themselves. Through regular participation in Sharing Circles, all of these goals can be realized.

When used regularly, the *process* of the Sharing Circle coupled with its *content* (specific discussion topics) provides students with frequent opportunities to become more aware of their strengths, abilities, and positive qualities. In the Sharing Circle, students are listened to when they express their feelings and ideas, and they learn to listen to each other. The Sharing Circle format provides a framework in which genuine attention and acceptance can be given and received on a consistent basis.

The process of verbal interaction is a key avenue to maintaining and enhancing mental health and well-being. Our emotional and intellectual lives are so complex that we would be devastated if we couldn't discuss our experiences with one another. When we share our experiences and feelings at a level beyond superficiality, we come to realize that all of us experience all of the emotions, but each of us experiences them in our own unique way. By sharing our experiences and feelings in a safe environment, we are able to see basic commonalties among human beings—and individual differences, too. This understanding contributes to the development of self-respect. On a foundation of self-respect, we then grow to understand and respect others, and in the process we develop the concern for humanity that is necessary to our becoming responsible members of the human family.

As an instructional tool, the purpose of the Sharing Circle is to promote growth and development in students of all ages. Targeted growth areas include **communication, self-aware-ness, personal mastery**, and **interpersonal skills**. As students follow the rules and relate to each other verbally during the Sharing Circle, they are practicing oral communication and learning to listen. Through insights developed in the course of pondering and discussing the various topics, students are offered the opportunity to grow in awareness and to feel more masterful—more in control of their feelings, thoughts, and behaviors. Through the positive experience of give and take, they learn more about effective modes of social interaction. The Sharing Circle provides practice in the use of basic communication skills while relevant life issues are being discussed and valuable concepts learned.

The Value of Listening

Many of us do not realize that merely listening to students talk can be immensely facilitating to their personal development. We do not need to diagnose, probe, or problem solve to help students focus attention on their own needs and use the information and insights in their own minds to arrive at their own conclusions. Because being listened to gives students confidence in their ability to positively affect their own lives, listening is certainly the helping method with the greatest long-term payoff.

When a student is dealing with a problem, or when her emotional state clearly indicates that something is bothering her, active listening is irreplaceable as a means of helping; however, we as helpers must be willing to set aside our own needs at the moment. Temporarily clearing our minds and neutralizing our biases allows us to concentrate fully on what is being said. In contrast, if we feel compelled to show we have the answer, or need to let the student know she did the wrong thing and is somehow deficient or inept, we will not be listening. Active listening puts us in the *student's* shoes while *she* does the walking. It communicates two messages: understanding and acceptance. It is based upon our knowing that the student is the only one who can solve her own problems. She has the most data about what is at issue and, if she can draw a solution from this data, she will have grown a step toward responsible adulthood.

It is important to remember that solutions do not generally come through a single big insight. Finding THE answer is not what usually happens on the path of personal development. A solution to a problem may be as simple as gaining a new perspective. Problem solving is a process that we must learn to do for ourselves our whole life long.

The Sharing Circle provides the opportunity for students to talk while others actively listen. By being given this opportunity on a daily basis, students gain important life skills and self-knowledge. Once they see that we do not intend to change them and that they may speak freely without threat of being "wrong," students find it easier to examine themselves and begin to see areas where they can make positive change in their lives. Just through the consistent process of sharing in a safe environment, students develop the ability to clarify their thoughts. They are encouraged to go deeper, find their own direction, and express and face strong feelings that may at other times be hidden obstacles to their growth. The important point is that students really can solve their own problems, develop self-awareness, and learn skills that assist them in becoming responsible members of society *if they are listened to effectively.*

Just as the Sharing Circle provides a process for students to learn about themselves through self-expression and exploration, it also teaches students how to *be* good listeners. The rules of the Sharing Circle (listening to the person who is speaking, without probing, put-downs, or gossip) and the periodic review demand that each student give active attention to the speaker. Through the regular practice of good listening skills and the positive modeling of active listening by the teacher or counselor leading the circle, the students begin to internalize good listening habits.

The key to all of this is, of course, regular participation in the Sharing Circle process. Skills and knowledge are developed over time through regular, sustained involvement in Sharing Circles. These benefits are the same for all ages from elementary through high school and beyond.

Awareness

Words are the only tool we have for systematically turning our attention and awareness to the feelings within us, and for describing and reflecting on our thoughts and behaviors. When we inwardly sense an idea we can't put into words, we struggle to *find* the words. Without words, we can't deal with the idea, share it with others, or clarify its meaning for ourselves. The effective use of words constitutes the first step in developing the ability to grasp previously unspoken feelings and understand the connection between feelings and behavior. Feelings, after all, lead people to marry, to seek revenge, to launch war, to create great works of art, and to commit their lives to the service of others. They are vital and compelling.

For students to be able to manage their feelings, they must know what those feelings are. To know what they are, they must practice describing them in words. When a particular feeling is grasped in words several times, the mind soon begins to automatically recall ideas and concepts in association with the feeling and can start to provide ways of dealing with the feeling; e.g., "I'm feeling angry and I need to get away from this situation to calm down."

With practice, the mind becomes more and more adept at making these connections. When a recognized feeling comes up, the mind can sort through alternative responses to the feeling. As a student practices this response sequence in reaction to a variety of feelings, he will find words floating into consciousness that accurately identify what is going on emotionally and physically for him. This knowledge in turn develops the capacity to think before and during action. One mark of maturity is the ability to recognize one's feelings and to take appropriate, responsible action. The more *immature* the student, the more his feelings rather than his thoughts determine his behavior. The ability to put words to feelings, to understand those words, to sort through an internal repertoire of responses and to choose appropriate, responsible behavior in reaction to a feeling indicates a high level of maturity and self-awareness.

By participating in Sharing Circles, students have many opportunities to focus on their feelings, thoughts, and behaviors, and those of others. Through regular verbal sharing, they develop an awareness of their feelings, they talk about their responses, and they listen to how others have responded in similar situations. Their repertoire of feeling words increases as does their ability to differentiate between appropriate and inappropriate behaviors. By verbally exploring their own experiences in the circle and listening to others do the same, all in an environment of safety, students are gently and gradually prompted to explore deeper within themselves and to grow and expand in their understanding of others. As this mutual sharing takes place, they learn that feelings, thoughts, and behaviors are real and experienced by everyone. They see others succeeding and failing in the same kinds of ways they succeed and fail. They also begin to see each person as unique and to realize that they are unique, too. Out of this understanding, students experience a growing concern for others. A sense of responsibility develops as the needs, problems, values, and preferences of others penetrate their awareness. Through the circle's regular sharing of ideas, hopes, dreams, fears, experiences, etc., students are provided an extraordinary opportunity to develop into caring, responsible, aware individuals.

Personal Mastery

Personal mastery can be defined as **self-confidence** together with **responsible competence**. Self-confidence is believing in oneself as a capable human being. Responsible competence is the willingness to take responsibility for one's actions coupled with the ability to demonstrate fundamental human relations skills (competencies).

Self-confident people believe in themselves and perceive themselves as being "okay." They are willing to try new challenges, are not debilitated by knowledge of their weaknesses, and do not strongly fear failure. Generally speaking, people with a high sense of personal mastery or high self-esteem are the ones who continue to succeed and, the more they succeed, the more they believe in themselves. Thus a beneficial cycle is established.

Individuals are likely to achieve personal mastery in their endeavors when they have a *feeling* of mastery about themselves. It's important to note that it is not what a person *does* that makes her self-confident, but rather her *attitude* toward what she does, which greatly depends on the attitudes of others toward her. The responses of significant others to what we do play a critical role in determining whether or not we see ourselves as masterful. If significant others in our lives let us know that they notice our efforts and comment positively to us when we try or succeed, our awareness of our capabilities *increases*. Conversely, without favorable comment we are *less* aware of our capabilities.

Through participation in Sharing Circles, students are gradually and systematically encouraged to explore their successes and hear positive comments about their efforts. Many Sharing Circle topics heighten students' awareness of their own successes and those of others. Failure, or falling short, is a reality that is also examined. The focus, however, is not to remind students that they have failed; instead these topics enable students to see that falling short is common and universal and is experienced by all people when they strive to accomplish things.

Sharing circle topics often address **human relations competencies**, such as the ability to include others, assume and share responsibility, offer help, behave assertively, resolve conflicts, solve problems, etc. Such topics elevate awareness in the human relations domain and encourage students to more effectively exercise these competencies and skills each day. The first step in a student's developing any competency is knowing that he or she is capable of demonstrating it. The Sharing Circle is particularly adept at helping students to recognize and acknowledge their own capabilities.

It is important to note that any topic can lead to a success experience if the student's contribution is well received. In the Sharing Circle, topics are interpreted and addressed at a personal level. They are made relevant to the individual and are therefore powerful catalysts for learning. The rules of the Sharing Circle create an atmosphere of freedom in which students can explore new behaviors and risk talking about their ideas a little more each day. Students feel encouraged to expand their repertoire of skills and competencies.

A particularly important element of personal mastery is **responsible competence**, or responsibility. By focusing on their positive behaviors and accomplishments, the attention of students is directed toward the internal and external rewards that can be gained when they behave responsibly.

The Sharing Circle is a wonderful tool for teaching cooperation. As equitably as possible, the circle structure attempts to meet the needs of all participants. Everyone's feelings are accepted. Comparisons and judgements are not made. The circle is not another competitive arena, but is guided by a spirit of collaboration. When students practice fair, respectful interaction with one another, they benefit from the experience and are likely to employ these responsible behaviors in other life situations.

Interpersonal Skills

Relating effectively to others is a challenge we all face. People who are effective in their social interactions have the ability to understand others. They know how to interact flexibly, skillfully, and responsibly. At the same time, they recognize their own needs and maintain their own integrity. Socially effective people can process the nonverbal as well as verbal messages of others. They possess the very important awareness that all people have the power to affect one another. They are aware of not only how others affect them, but the effects their behaviors have on others.

In order to build healthy relationships, students need to have positive interpersonal experiences and to gain information concerning the social realm of life. However, we generally have no way of systematically teaching young people how to understand and get along with other people.

The Sharing Circle process has been designed so that healthy, responsible behaviors are modeled by the teacher or counselor in his or her role as circle leader. The rules also require that the students relate positively and effectively to one another. The Sharing Circle brings out and affirms the positive qualities inherent in everyone and allows students to practice effective modes of communication. Through regular practice and reinforcement, students internalize effective interpersonal skills and are then able to transfer those skills to other situations. Because Sharing Circles provide a place where participants are listened to and their feelings accepted, students learn how to provide the same conditions to peers and adults outside the circle.

One of the great benefits of the Sharing Circle is that it does not merely *teach* young people about social interaction, it lets them *interact!* Every Sharing Circle is a real-life experience of social interaction where the students share, listen, explore, plan, dream, and problem solve together. As they interact, they learn about each other and they realize what it takes to relate effectively to others. Any given Sharing Circle may provide a dozen tiny flashes of positive interpersonal insight for an individual participant. Gradually, the reality of what constitutes effective behavior in relating to others is internalized.

Through this regular sharing of interpersonal experiences, the students learn that behavior can be positive or negative, and sometimes both at the same time. Consequences can be constructive, destructive, or both. Different people respond differently to the same event. They have different feelings and thoughts. The students begin to understand what will cause what to happen; they grasp the concept of cause and effect; they see themselves affecting others and being affected *by* others.

The ability to make accurate interpretations and responses in social interactions, when combined with growing self-knowledge and awareness, produces a broad and practical sense of values or ethics. When students possess this ability, they know where they stand with themselves and with others. They can tell what actions "fit" a situation. Sharing circles are marvelous testing grounds where students can observe themselves and others in action, and can begin to see themselves as contributing to the

How to Set Up Sharing Circles

Group Size and Composition

Sharing Circles are a time for focusing on individuals' contributions in an unhurried fashion. For this reason, each circle session group needs to be kept relatively small—eight to twelve usually works best. Once they move beyond the primary grades, students are capable of extensive verbalization. You will want to encourage this, and not stifle them because of time constraints.

Each group should be as **heterogeneous** as possible with respect to sex, ability, and racial/ethnic background. Sometimes there will be a group in which all the students are particularly reticent to speak. At these times, bring in an expressive student or two who will get things going. Sometimes it is necessary for practical reasons to change the membership of a group. Once established, however, it is advisable to keep a group as stable as possible.

Length and Location of Sharing Circles

Most circle sessions last approximately 20 to 30 minutes. At first students tend to be reluctant to express themselves fully because they do not yet know that the circle is a safe place. Consequently your first sessions may not last more than 10 to 15 minutes. Generally speaking, students become comfortable and motivated to speak with continued experience.

In secondary classrooms circle sessions may be conducted at any time during the class period. Starting circle sessions at the beginning of the period allows additional time in case students become deeply involved in the topic. If you start circles late in the period, make sure the students are aware of their responsibility to be concise.

In elementary classes, any time of day is appropriate for Sharing Circles. Some teachers like to set the tone for the day by beginning with circles; others feel it's a perfect way to complete the day and to send the children away with positive feelings.

Circle sessions may be carried out wherever there is room for students to sit in a circle and experience few or no distractions. Most leaders prefer to have students sit in chairs rather than on the floor. Students seem to be less apt to invade one another's space while seated in chairs. Some leaders conduct sessions outdoors, with students seated in a secluded, grassy area.

How to Get Started

Teachers and counselors have used numerous methods to involve students in the circle process. What works well for one leader or class does not always work for another. Here are two basic strategies leaders have successfully used to set up groups. Whichever you use, we recommend that you post a chart listing the circle session rules and procedures to which every participant may refer.

1. Start one group at a time, and cycle through all groups. If possible, provide an opportunity for every student to experience a circle session in a setting where there are no disturbances. This may mean arranging for another staff member or aide to take charge of the students not participating in the circle. Nonparticipants may work on course work or silent reading, or, if you have a cooperative librarian, they may be sent to the library to work independently or in small groups on a class assignment. Repeat this procedure until all of the students have been involved in at least one circle session.

Next, initiate a class discussion about the circle sessions. Explain that from now on you will be meeting with each circle group in the classroom, with the remainder of the class present. Ask the students to help you plan established procedures for the remainder of the class to follow.

Meet with each circle session group on a different day, systematically cycling through the groups. In grades 3 and up, you may wish to start student leadership training after you've completed a number of circles. In each group, allow a student the opportunity to lead the session as you sit beside him or her, acting as leader-trainer. In time, student-led groups may meet independently at staggered times during the period, or they may meet simultaneously in different parts of the room while you circulate. Eventually you should be able to be a participant in the student-led groups. For more information on student leadership, refer to the next chapter, "Training Student Leaders."

2. Combine inner and outer circles. Meet with one circle session group while another group listens and observes as an outer circle. Then have the two groups change places, with the students on the outside becoming the inner circle, and responding verbally to the topic. If you run out of time in secondary classrooms, use two class periods for this. Later, a third group may be added to this alternating cycle. The end product of this arrangement is two or more groups (comprising everyone in the class) meeting together simultaneously. While one group is involved in discussion, the other groups listen and observe as members of an outer circle. *Invite the members of the outer circle to participate in the review and discussion phases of the circle.*

What To Do With the Rest of the Class

A number of arrangements can be made for students who are not participating in circle sessions. Here are some ideas:

- **Arrange the room to ensure privacy.** This may involve placing a circle of chairs or carpeting in a corner, away from other work areas. You might construct dividers from existing furniture, such as bookshelves or screens, or simply arrange chairs and tables in such a way that the circle area is protected from distractions.

- **Involve aides, counselors, parents, or fellow teachers.** Have an aide conduct a lesson with the rest of the class while you meet with a circle group. If you do not have an aide assigned to you, use auxiliary staff or parent volunteers.

- **Have students work quietly on subject-area assignments in pairs or small, task-oriented groups.**

- **Utilize student aides or leaders.** If the seat-work activity is in a content area, appoint students who show ability in that area as "consultants," and have them assist other students.

- **Give the students plenty to do.** List academic activities on the board. Make materials for quiet individual activities available so that students cannot run out of things to do and be tempted to consult you or disturb others.

- **Make the activity of students outside the circle enjoyable.** When you can involve the rest of the class in something meaningful to them, students will probably be less likely to interrupt the circle.

- **Have the students work on an ongoing project.** When they have a task in progress, students can simply resume where they left off, with little or no introduction from you. In these cases, appointing a "person in charge," "group leader," or "consultant" is wise.

- **Allow individual journal-writing.** While a circle is in progress, have the other students make entries in a private (or share-with-teacher-only) journal. The topic for journal writing could be the same topic that is being discussed in the Sharing Circle. Do not correct the journals, but if you read them, be sure to respond to the entries with your own written thoughts, where appropriate.

Leading the Sharing Circle

This section is a thorough guide for conducting Sharing Circles. It covers major points to keep in mind and answers questions which will arise as you begin using the program. Please remember that these guidelines are presented to assist you, not to restrict you. Follow them and trust your own leadership style at the same time.

Sharing Circle Procedures for the Leader

1. **Setting up the circle** (1-2 minutes)
2. **Reviewing the ground rules** (1-2 minutes) *
3. **Introducing the topic** (1-2 minutes)
4. **Sharing by circle members** (12-18 minutes)
5. **Reviewing what is shared** (3-5 minutes) **
6. **Summary discussion** (2-8 minutes)
7. **Closing the circle** (less than 1 minute)
   *optional after the first few sessions
   **optional

Setting up the circle (1-2 minutes)

As you sit down with the students in the circle, remember that you are not teaching a lesson. You are facilitating a group of people. Establish a positive atmosphere. In a relaxed manner, address each student by name, using eye contact and conveying warmth. An attitude of seriousness blended with enthusiasm will let the students know that the circle session is an important learning experience—an activity that can be interesting and meaningful.

Reviewing the ground rules (1-2 minutes).

At the beginning of the first session, and at appropriate intervals thereafter, go over the rules for the circle session. They are:

Sharing Circle Rules

1. **Bring yourself to the circle and nothing else.**
2. **Everyone gets a turn to share, including the leader.**
3. **You can skip your turn if you wish.**
4. **Listen to the person who is sharing.**
5. **The time is shared equally.**
6. **Stay in your own space.**
7. **There are no interruptions, probing, put-downs, or gossip.**

From this point on, demonstrate to the students that you expect them to remember and abide by the ground rules. Convey that you think well of them and know they are fully capable of responsible behavior. Let them know that by coming to the session they are making a commitment to listen and show acceptance and respect for the other students and you.

Introducing the topic (1-2 minutes)

State the topic in your own words. Elaborate and provide examples as each activity suggests. Add clarifying statements of your own that will help the students understand the topic. Answer questions about the topic, and emphasize that there are no "right" responses. Finally, restate the topic, opening the session to responses (theirs and yours). Sometimes taking your turn first helps the students understand the aim of the topic. At various points throughout the session, state the topic again.

Just prior to leading a circle session, contemplate the topic and think of at least one possible response that *you* can make to it.

Sharing by circle members (12-18 minutes)

The most important point to remember is this: The purpose of the circle session is to give students an opportunity to express themselves and be accepted for the experiences, thoughts, and feelings they share. Avoid taking the action away from the circle members. They are the stars!

Reviewing what is shared (optional 3-5 minutes)

Besides modeling effective listening (the very best way to teach it) and positively reinforcing students for attentive listening, a review can be used to deliberately improve listening skills in circle members.

Reviewing is a time for reflective listening, when circle members feed back what they heard each other say during the sharing phase of the circle. Besides encouraging effective listening, reviewing provides circle members with additional recognition. It validates their experience and conveys the idea, "you are important," a message we can all profit from hearing often.

To review, a circle member simply addresses someone who shared, and briefly paraphrases what the person said ("John, I heard you say...").

The first few times you conduct reviews, stress the importance of checking with the speaker to see if the review accurately summarized the main things that were shared. If the speaker says, "No," allow him or her to make corrections. Stress too, the importance of speaking *directly* to the speaker, using the person's name and the pronoun "you," not "he" or "she." If someone says, "She said that...," intervene as promptly and respectfully as possible and say to the reviewer, "Talk to Betty...Say you." This is very important. The person whose turn is being reviewed will have a totally different feeling when talked *to*, instead of *about.*

Note: Remember that the review is optional and is most effective when used *occasionally*, not as a part of every circle.

Summary discussion (2-8 minutes)

The summary discussion is the cognitive portion of the circle session. During this phase, the leader asks thought-provoking questions to stimulate free discussion and higher-level thinking. Each circle session in this book includes summary questions; however, at times you may want to formulate questions that are more appropriate to the level of understanding in your group— or to what was actually shared in the circle. If you wish to make connections between the circle session topic and your content area, ask questions that will accomplish that objective and allow the summary discussion to extend longer.

It is important that you not confuse the summary with the review. The review is optional; the summary is not. The summary meets the need of people of all ages to find meaning in what they do. Thus, the summary serves as a necessary culmination to each circle session by allowing the students to clarify the key concepts they gained from the session.

Closing the circle (less than 1 minute).

The ideal time to end a circle session is when the summary discussion reaches natural closure. Sincerely thank everyone for being part of the circle. Don't thank specific students for speaking, as doing so might convey the impression that speaking is more appreciated than mere listening. Then close the circle by saying, "The circle session is over," or "OK, that ends our session."

More about Sharing Circle Procedures and Rules

The next few paragraphs offer further clarification concerning circle session leadership.

Why should students bring themselves to the circle and nothing else? Individual teachers differ on this point, but most prefer that students not bring objects (such as pencils, books, etc.) to the circle that may be distracting.

Who gets to talk? Everyone. The importance of acceptance in Sharing Circles cannot be overly stressed. In one way or another practically every ground rule says one thing: *accept one another.* When you model acceptance of students, they will learn how to be accepting. Each individual in the circle is important and deserves a turn to speak if he or she wishes to take it. Equal opportunity to become involved should be given to everyone in the circle.

Circle members should be reinforced equally for their contributions. There are many reasons why a leader may become more enthused over what one student shares than another. The response may be more on target, reflect more depth, be more entertaining, be philosophically more in keeping with one's own point of view, and so on. However, students need to be given equal recognition for their contributions, even if the contribution is to listen silently throughout the session.

In most of the circle sessions, plan to take a turn and address the topic, too. Students usually appreciate it very much and learn a great deal when their teachers and counselors are willing to tell about their own experiences, thoughts, and feelings. In this way you let your students know that you acknowledge your own humanness.

Does everyone have to take a turn? No. Students may choose to skip their turns. If the circle becomes a pressure situation in which the members are coerced in any way to speak, it will become an unsafe place where participants are not comfortable. Meaningful discussion is unlikely in such an atmosphere. By allowing students to make this choice, you are showing them that you accept their right to remain silent if that is what they choose to do.

As you begin circles, it will be to your advantage if one or more students decline to speak. If you are imperturbable and accepting when this happens, you let them know you are offering them an opportunity to experience something you think is valuable, or at least worth a try, and not attempting to force-feed them. You as a leader should not feel compelled to share a personal experience in every session, either. However, if you decline to speak in most of the sessions, this may have an inhibiting effect on the students' willingness to share.

A word should also be said about how this ground rule has sometimes been carried to extremes. Sometimes leaders have bent over backwards to let students know they don't have to take a turn. This seeming lack of enthusiasm on the part of the leader has caused reticence in the students. In order to avoid this outcome, don't project any personal insecurity as you lead the session. Be confident in your proven ability to work with students. Expect something to happen and it will.

Some circle leaders ask the participants to raise their hands when they wish to speak, while others simply allow free verbal sharing without soliciting the leader's permission first. Choose the procedure that works best for you, but do not call on anyone unless you can see signs of readiness.

Some leaders have reported that their first circles fell flat— that no one, or just one or two students, had anything to say. But they continued to have circles, and at a certain point everything changed. Thereafter, the students had a great deal to say that these leaders considered worth waiting for. It appears that in these cases the leaders' acceptance of the right to skip turns was a key factor. In time most students will contribute verbally when they have something they want to say, and when they are assured there is no pressure to do so.

Sometimes a silence occurs during a circle session. Don't feel you have to jump in every time someone stops talking. During silences students have an opportunity to think about what they would like to share or to contemplate an important idea they've heard. A general rule of thumb is to allow silence to the point that you observe group discomfort. At that point move on. *Do not switch to another topic.* To do so implies you will not be satisfied until the students speak. If you change to another topic, you are telling them you didn't really mean it when you said they didn't have to take a turn if they didn't want to.

If you are bothered about students who attend a number of circles and still do not share verbally, reevaluate what you consider to be involvement. Participation does not necessarily mean talking. Students who do not speak *are* listening and learning.

How can I encourage effective listening? The Sharing Circle is a time (and place) for students and leaders to strengthen the habit of listening by doing it over and over again. No one was born knowing how to listen effectively to others. It is a skill like any other that gets better as it is practiced. In the immediacy of the circle session, the members become keenly aware of the necessity to listen, and most students respond by expecting it of one another.

In the Sharing Circle, listening is defined as the respectful focusing of attention on individual speakers. It includes eye contact with the speaker and open body posture. It eschews interruptions of any kind. When you conduct a circle session, listen and encourage listening in the students by (1) focusing your attention on the person who is speaking, (2) being receptive to what the speaker is saying (not mentally planning your next remark), and (3) recognizing the speaker when she finishes speaking, either verbally ("Thanks, Shirley") or nonverbally (a nod and a smile).

To encourage effective listening in the students, reinforce them by letting them know you have noticed they were listening to each other and you appreciate it. Occasionally conducting a review after the sharing phase also has the effect of sharpening listening skills.

How can I ensure the students get equal time? When circle members share the time equally, they demonstrate their acceptance of the notion that everyone's contribution is of equal importance. It is not uncommon to have at least one dominator in a group. This person is usually totally unaware that by continuing to talk he or she is taking time from others who are less assertive.

Be very clear with the students about the purpose of this ground rule. Tell them at the outset how much time there is and whether or not you plan to conduct a review. When it is your turn, always limit your own contribution. If someone goes on and on, do intervene (dominators need to know what they are doing), but do so as gently and respectfully as you can.

What are some examples of put-downs? Put-downs convey the message, "You are not okay as you are." Some put-downs are deliberate, but many are made unknowingly. Both kinds are undesirable in a Sharing Circle because they destroy the atmosphere of acceptance and disrupt the flow of discussion. Typical put-downs include:

- overquestioning.
- statements that have the effect of teaching or preaching
- advice giving
- one-upsmanship
- criticism, disapproval, or objections
- sarcasm
- statements or questions of disbelief

How can I deal with put-downs? There are two major ways for dealing with put-downs in circle sessions: preventing them from occurring and intervening when they do.

Going over the ground rules with the students at the beginning of each session, particularly in the earliest sessions, is a helpful preventive technique. Another is to reinforce the students when they adhere to the rule. Be sure to use nonpatronizing, nonevaluative language.

Unacceptable behavior should be stopped the moment it is recognized by the leader. When you become aware that a put-dcwn is occurring, do whatever you ordinarily do to stop destructive behavior in the classroom. If one student gives another an unasked-for bit of advice, say for example, "Jane, please give Alicia a chance to tell her story." To a student who interrupts say, "Ed, it's Sally's turn." In most cases the fewer words, the better—students automatically tune out messages delivered as lectures.

Sometimes students disrupt the group by starting a private conversation with the person next to them. Touch the offender on the arm or shoulder while continuing to give eye contact to the student who is speaking. If you can't reach the offender, simply remind him or her of the rule about listening. If students persist in putting others down during circle sessions, ask to see them at another time and hold a brief one-to-one conference, urging them to follow the rules. Suggest that they reconsider their membership in the circle. Make it clear that if they don't intend to honor the ground rules, they are not to come to the circle.

How can I keep students from gossiping? Periodically remind students that using names and sharing embarrassing information is not acceptable. Urge the students to relate personally to one another, but not to tell intimate details of their lives.

What should the leader do during the summary discussion? Conduct the summary as an open forum, giving students the opportunity to discuss a variety of ideas and accept those that make sense to them. Don't impose your opinions on the students, or allow the students to impose theirs on one another. Ask open-ended questions, encourage higher-level thinking, contribute your own ideas when appropriate, and act as a facilitator.

Training Student Leaders

A basic assumption of the Sharing Circle process is that every human being (barring those having considerable subnormal intelligence) has leadership potential. Further, the best time for energizing this ability is in childhood, and the optimum time for maintaining the skills is during adolescence. Students in countless elementary and secondary classrooms effectively lead their own circle sessions.

You can begin training student leaders after two or three successful circle sessions. Invite the students to consider volunteering to lead a Sharing Circle. Suggest that they watch you closely to see what steps the leader follows. At the end of the session, ask the students to describe what you did. They should be able to delineate the following steps:

The leader:
1. announces the topic and clarifies what it is about.
2. may lead a review of the ground rules.
3. gives each person a turn who wants one.
4. may conduct a review of what each person said.
5. conducts a summary discussion by focusing on the meaning of the session and the major observations of the participants.
6. terminates the circle.

Ask the students if anyone would like to volunteer to lead the next session. If no one volunteers, accept this outcome and wait for a session or two before trying again. If several volunteer, choose a student who you think is very likely to succeed. Then tell the group the topic you have in mind for the next session.

Before the next session, give the student leader a copy of the activity, and discuss it with him or her. Also provide a copy of the Sharing Circle rules and procedures (see "**Leading the Sharing Circle**"). As the session begins, tell the group that you will be the trainer and speak about the process when necessary, but that otherwise, the student is the leader and you are a participant. Before turning the session over to the student leader add one more thing—a new ground rule stating that the students are expected to respect fully the leadership position of the student. **If they disagree with the student leader's procedure or are aware of what he or she should do next when the student leader may have forgotten, they are not to say anything at that time unless they are asked to by the student leader.** When people are learning a new skill, it can be very upsetting to have other people constantly reminding them of what they are supposed to do next. For this reason the student leader should not be heckled in any way. (Time can be taken at the end of the session for the group to give feedback and to thank the student leader for his or her performance).

Now, allow the student leader to proceed, interjecting statements yourself about the procedure only when absolutely necessary. Be sure to take your turn and model respectful listening. As necessary, deal with students who interrupt or distract the group.

Before ending the session, thank the student leader, and conduct a brief feedback session by asking the students, "Who would like to tell (the student leader) what you liked about the way he or she conducted the session?" Let the student leader call on each person who has a comment.

Tell the students the topic you have in mind for the next session, and ask for a volunteer to lead it. Remember that students should not lead the group until you are sure they will be successful. Be careful to appoint leaders of both sexes and all racial/ethnic groups. Continue this process until all who wish to conduct a Sharing Circle are competent enough to lead them independently.

Combining Teacher and Student Leadership

This procedure allows several groups to meet simultaneously.

Begin by announcing to the class that you will be leading part of the Sharing Circle with the entire class and then they will break into their individual circles and complete them with students leading. If necessary, review the ground rules with the whole class. Then announce the topic, describe it and restate it. Finally, take your turn to relate to it personally. Answer any questions the students have, and then ask them to get into their groups.

When the circles are formed, the student leaders take over. They restate the topic and facilitate the sharing phase and, if desired, a review. The students return to their regular seating for the summary discussion, which is led by the teacher.

Note: This is a particularly fruitful procedure if you are using Sharing Circles as supplements to your regular subject. The summary discussion can then include questions concerning the relevancy of the topic to subject matter currently being studied (see, **"Creating Your Own Sharing Circle Topics"**).

Creating Your Own Sharing Circle Topics

Because Sharing Circles can be adapted to almost any situation and have such a wide range of positive outcomes, it is useful to understand the approach to creating them.

How Sharing Circle Topics Are Developed

Topics in the Sharing Circle program are presented according to a principle of learning that has been validated in a wide variety of applications. This principle is called *successive approximation*, and simply means, *begin where learners are or where they are likely to be and proceed to steps that are in keeping with the learners' progress*. The program is designed to help students develop useful insights into themselves and others while they practice positive communication skills. Circle session topics are experiential approximations of those insights.

Generally speaking, it is relatively easy to talk about things past and less easy to talk about right now. Second, it is typically easier to talk about other people and less easy to talk about oneself. Third, it seems to be easier for most people to talk about behavior than to talk about feelings. Finally, pleasant emotions are easier for most people to describe than negative ones. The examples that follow indicate topics at each end of the continuum for each of the four dimensions.

1. **Past** ....**Present**
   "A Pleasant Memory"   "Something I Feel Good
                                              About Today"

2. **Other People** ....**Self**
   "Someone Did Something for   "A Way I Take Care of
   Someone Else"   Myself"

3. **Behavior** ....**Feelings**
   "I Helped Someone Who Needed   "A Time I Felt Shy"
   and Wanted My Help"

4. **Positive Feelings** ....**Negative Feelings**
   "Something That Makes   "Something That Makes
   Me Feel Good"   Me Feel Sad"

Thoughts on Developing Your Own Topics

Many teachers and students generate topics tailor-made to fit their needs. If these topics are generated so that the less complex are presented first, moving sequentially toward the more complex, the principle of learning underlying the program will be maintained. Insights may come anywhere along the continuum, but they are more likely to occur when students are on familiar ground. The test of ease for a topic will be the sharing in the circle. Here are three other points to keep in mind:

1. **If you create a topic that relates to an issue of some kind, remember that in issue-oriented Sharing Circles there need be no agreement.** The Sharing Circle is not a rap session. Each person merely voices his or her own thoughts and feelings about the issue. The emphasis is on listening to one another's remarks and becoming aware of one's own thoughts and feelings. During the summary discussion, elicit comments from the students on the similarities and differences in their feelings and thoughts and ask open-ended, thought-provoking questions.

2. **Do not initiate a topic that might be a lead-in for ax-grinding on the part of you or anyone else in the circle.** If you need to express strong feelings to the students, find another method. The same principle applies to a situation in which one or more students have some strong feelings to express to each other. *The Sharing Circle is not a setting for confrontation, not even subtle confrontation!*

3. **Make sure that the topic, when it is discussed, will lead to an exploration of feelings.** If you hold circle sessions and feelings are not discussed, they are not Sharing Circles.

Guidelines for Developing Sharing Circle Topics

Formulate topics in light of the considerations already mentioned. To avoid the repetitious "A Time...," other starters for topics are:

"When..."	"An Idea I..."
"One of..."	"The Way..."
"Something I..."	"How..."
"What..."	"Things I..."
"One Way..."	"The Thing That..."

Consider what you are trying to achieve with the topic. Does it relate to one of the three growth areas, Awareness, Personal Mastery, or Interpersonal Skills? Is it in harmony with other aspects of your curriculum?

Be sure to present the topic to the students in an open-ended manner. Elaborate on it. Mention suggestions and possibilities to help them start thinking about it. State the topic at the beginning of your introduction and again at the end.

As you listen to students respond, do not feel compelled to question them. If you do ask a question, be sure it's open-ended and asked with the intention of helping them express themselves more fully. In general, questions asked to students when they are sharing should help students develop an awareness of **feelings**, their own and others. For example:

— Do you remember how you felt at the time?
— How do you feel about that now?

Questions may enable students to become more aware of their **behavior**.

— Do you remember what you said/did when it happened?
— How did other people act/react in that situation?

Questions may help students focus on their own **thoughts**, including attitudes, beliefs, preferences, etc., to learn more about how their thoughts influence their feelings and behavior.

— Did any thought or image cross your mind when that happened?
— Do you remember how that idea caused you to feel or act?

Guidelines for Developing Summary Discussion Questions.

The purpose of the summary is to involve students intellectually, to encourage them to examine the implications of what they have shared, and to stimulate higher-order thinking skills. The summary starters listed below relate to Awareness, Personal Mastery, and Interpersonal Skills.

Awareness

— What kinds of things do people do...?
— If you feel...does that mean...?
— What is it that...?
— What kinds of things do...?
— When people...?
— If you want..., then...?

Personal Mastery

— How can a person...?
— Do you think...should have to...?
— What can you do when...?
— Is it too early/late to...?

Interpersonal Skills

— If you want people to..., then...?
— Would all of us...?
— Are there ways we...?
— Are there times when...?
— What can you say to...?

Questions and Answers

Here is a collection of answers to the most frequently asked questions about Sharing Circles. They are categorized into the leader's role, classroom management, student responses, and process and content.

Questions About the Leader's Role While Conducting Circle Sessions

1. How long will I feel strange and awkward using the process of the Sharing Circle?

The Sharing Circle may demand behaviors from you that feel unnatural. It is important to remember that these procedures were developed because of their proven effectiveness in promoting positive communication skills in students. You are urged to follow the format, to keep interaction positive, and to serve as an effective communication model. Use your own personal style. So long as the basic circle session procedures are followed, your style should reflect what is most comfortable and closest to the real you.

2. Do I have to share verbally in the circle session?

The ground rules apply to everyone equally: all the participants get a turn to speak, but they don't have to take it. Hence, there may be a number of times when you will choose not to share. On the other hand, if you rarely share, the students will probably not see you as a real member of the group. They may begin to respond with what they think you want to hear, not their real thoughts and feelings.

3. How long should I wait for a student to share verbally the first time?

Until he or she shares. Re-evaluate what you consider to be involvement. Participation may be something other than talking. Attentiveness to others is positive participation. Verbal sharing is likely to occur when students feel comfortable, secure, and included and when they have something to say. Most teachers indicate this is generally not a serious problem in their circles after the students have experienced two or more sessions.

4. What should I do if I forget who said what during a circle session?

Be honest and ask for help. Your honesty sends the message: "It's okay to forget; everybody does. Even teachers are human."

5. There are times when I can make a very important moral or value point from the sharing that occurs in the circle. What should I do?

The basic atmosphere of the Sharing Circle is one of acceptance. Moralizing has a judgmental quality. If you feel you should make a value statement, use an "I" message. That is, own the statement as a reflection of your own position or society's position, as you see it. (For example: "I think it's not right for people to take things that don't belong to them." "It seems to me that most people don't like to be interrupted.") In addition, ask the students what they think about the issue during the summary discussion, and accept their responses.

6. What should I do about a parent who asks to observe a circle?

Invite all parents and community members openly and warmly to participate in the circle. Explain the ground rules for the session (or ask the students to explain them) with the understanding that the parents have a right to share if they desire to—the same right the students have in the Sharing Circle every day. Carry out the circle as you normally do, and take the time to answer the parents' questions afterward. The experience of participating in a Sharing Circle is generally a positive one and usually answers most questions parents have.

Questions about Classroom Management

7. When is the best time to begin implementing Sharing Circles with a particular group or class?

The best time to introduce Sharing Circles is when the class or group first forms. This usually occurs at the beginning of the school year. The program helps students get to know you and each other. Teachers who wait for a few weeks before introducing Sharing Circles are more likely to experience reticence in students than those who introduce the activities at the outset.

8. I like the idea, but I don't have the time. How can I fit Sharing Circles into my overloaded curriculum?

If you don't have the time, you can't! Your choice is "Shall I do Sharing Circles?" If you respond yes, you will find time. While you are leading circle sessions, other students are doing independent seat work on your subject matter.

9. How should I decide who will be in which group?

There are numerous ways. Choose the one you feel will work best for you. The important don'ts are: (1) don't ability-group; and (2) don't separate students according to sex or ethnicity. The maximum number should be 12, and eventually everyone in the entire class should participate in Sharing Circles.

10. Do students have to attend the Sharing Circle?

No. If a student is involved with a task that for him or her takes precedence over attending the Sharing Circle, then you may wish to allow that student to follow his or her own interests. On the other hand, if nonattendance is avoidance, you have a different situation. By avoiding, the student may be saying that he or she feels threatened, or uncomfortable, or that sharing is required. A solution may be to reassure the student that attendance does not have to mean verbal sharing. Everyone has the right to participate silently.

11. How should I introduce a new student to the Sharing Circle?

Many ways are open to you. You may have another student in the circle tell the new participant what's happening, what the ground rules are, and so on. Our experience indicates that introducing a new student to a small group facilitates acceptance in the larger group. New students have reported that the circles were especially helpful in allowing them to make friends in a new situation.

12. What should I do with the rest of the class while Sharing Circles are being carried out?

The same thing you do when you use other small-group activities in the classroom. You may assign a wide variety of seat work, including free reading, journal writing, catch-up time, individualized contracts, etc. This question is specifically dealt with earlier in the section.

13. How should I deal with resistant students?

Students are easily misinterpreted. Quite often their seeming hostility or impudence is a mask covering shyness and fear. You don't have to solve their problems, and your attentive listening to them shows you care. Should a student say, "But we're not learning anything!" your response may be along the following lines:

Teacher: "How do you communicate with people outside the classroom?"
Student: "Talk. "
Teacher: "What for?"
Student: "To find out what's happening."
Teacher: "Is talking taught in school?"
Student: "Yeah, sort of."
Teacher: "Then maybe you are learning something."

Questions About Student Responses in Circle Sessions:

14. What can I do if students look blank, or there are long silences?

This behavior is not unusual, particularly when you first start Sharing Circle sessions or if the topic is one students seldom think about. Suppose you sense the students are having difficulty grasping or relating to the topic. You can legitimize the silence by saying something like, "This topic requires some thought. Let's all take a minute to think about it."

Allow a minute or so to pass, restate the topic, and wait for someone to share. You may also decide to take your turn first if you sense the students would appreciate further clarification.

Another strategy is to announce the topic ahead of time, either the day before or at the beginning of the class period. You might also list topics on the chalkboard.

15. How should I respond when another member of the Sharing Circle laughs at or puts down the student who is sharing?

Respond by letting the student know that what he or she is doing is unacceptable. Your first responsibility is to protect the speaker, even if your response to the offender appears to be a put-down. When it is his or her turn to speak, you will protect him or her just as vigorously.

At appropriate intervals remind the students of the rules, and if the unacceptable behavior persists, *excuse* the student from the circle session.

16. How do I deal with a response that indicates a student enjoys hurting others?

First of all, be sure the response is an honest one and not designed to get attention. If it is the latter kind, do not reward it with attention. If it is an honest statement, you have several options. You may accept the response without comment (probably the most difficult for many teachers), you may send an "I" message ("Hurting others gives me a bad feeling."), or you may ask the student how she or he thinks the other person felt about it.

17. What should I do when one student copies the response of another?

Accept the response. You may say, "Would you like to tell us more about...?" so the response can be individualized. Remember that a copied response may indicate avoidance by an individual who does not feel secure. This usually occurs when circle sessions are begun. Wait. Time will gradually establish a feeling of security.

18. How do you stop someone from sharing and sharing and sharing?

Ask the individual a closed-ended question that calls for a succinct response. Another strategy is to interrupt as gracefully as possible so you may reflect on what has been shared so far. Then repeat the topic to enable someone else to respond. From time to time gently but firmly remind the group that everyone has a right to share and that the time is limited.

19. What should I do when I get highly emotional responses to a topic?

This will happen occasionally because we all feel strong

emotions at times. The vast majority of the Sharing Circle topics are upbeat and positive, but some zero in directly on negative emotions. When students respond very emotionally during the Sharing Circle, be sure to demonstrate acceptance of their feelings, and concern and caring for them. Do not feel compelled to cheer them up or solve their problems for them.

20. What do I do if a student starts crying during a circle?

First and foremost, accept the response positively as a legitimate expression of feeling. Let the student know that it is acceptable behavior. Everyone needs to cry at times. Give the student free, warm attention while he or she cries, and let him/her cry until he or she is finished. Tell the group, "Sharon is getting rid of her hurt by crying." If you model this behavior, the other students will behave similarly. If the student wishes to leave the circle, excuse him or her, but make contact again before the end of the class session.

21. What if a student starts telling about something negative that occurred involving another student in the circle?

This can usually be headed off during the beginning of the circle session by reminding students of the no-gossip rule. This is especially true if the topic can be used to get back at another student. Like any other rule, it needs to be enforced gently but firmly. This will remind students that the Sharing Circle is a special, protected environment.

22. What should I do if a student raises family problems as a response to a topic?

Students should be regularly reminded that naming names and sharing embarrassing information is not done in the Sharing Circle. If family problems are shared, accept the statement, but do not pursue it. If a student persists, it would appear she or he needs to talk with someone. A response to this issue that we especially like is, "I'm a bit uncomfortable talking about that here, but I'll talk with you about it later. Is that all right?"

23. What should I do about issues raised in a Sharing Circle such as anger or lying?

Sometimes a student will tell about feeling angry or talk about a time when someone lied and how he or she felt about it. While names should not be mentioned, this is a very acceptable part of a Sharing Circle because the student is sharing an experience and the feelings that went with it. However, angry confrontations in a Sharing Circle are not acceptable. If a confrontation occurs, remind the students that the Sharing Circle is not meant for confronting one another or putting each other down in any way. Provide an alternative outlet for students who wish to express anger or hostility. For example, you might suggest journal writing that is either private or shared only with the teacher.

24. What do you do when a student has lied in the Sharing Circle?

First, do not confront the student or allow his or her peers to do so. We suggest that you consider the reason for the exaggeration or lie, which is much more important than the lie itself. In reflecting on the reason consider the structure of the Sharing Circle. Do the students feel they have to share? Are experiences of an unusual nature the only kind of sharing that receives recognition?

Questions About the Process and Content of Sharing Circles

25. Is it all right to change the topic when it appears that no one will share?

We prefer that you not. Instead, reflect to yourself on the reasons for the lack of response. Perhaps something is getting in the way of trust-building between you and your students. If you consistently change topics until someone speaks, you are essentially sending this message: "I won't be satisfied until you talk," which stands in direct opposition to the rule of voluntary sharing.

26. How long should I allow a silence in a Sharing Circle to last?

Normally, continued silences are not a part of the classroom experience, although short silences do occur during some Sharing Circles. Consider if the silence is reflective thinking before you interrupt. A general rule of thumb is to allow silence to the point that you observe group discomfort. It may have a catalytic effect if you share your feelings about the silence or begin to respond to the topic yourself as a means of getting things going. If you have tried these things and the silence persists, you may indicate, "Today doesn't seem to be a good day for sharing. The next time we meet for a Sharing Circle, the topic will be..." Then stop the session.

27. Will having the Sharing Circle on a regular basis help my problem students?

If by problem students you mean those who consistently disrupt your scheduled activities by seeking attention and recognition, the circle can help, *if* they abide by the ground rules during the sessions. The Sharing Circle is not a panacea. It does provide a time and place for everyone to be given attention and recognition—a space where others will listen. We believe that eventually these factors make a difference in students and classrooms.

28. What should I do when issues are raised in a Sharing Circle that relate to cognitive themes in the curriculum?

If the students are interested in the issue, discuss it briefly, preferably as part of the summary discussion. Capitalize on their interest, but keep in mind that the Sharing Circle is not for instruction. If instruction begins to take place regularly during circle sessions, the students will lose that time for self-expression.

29. What should I do when sharing is really just beginning and the time is up?

First of all, be sure to hold the session when there is enough time to follow all the Sharing Circle procedures. If the time is up before everyone has had a chance to speak, end the Sharing Circle by expressing your appreciation to the students for listening and sharing. Remind them that soon there will be another chance to participate, and tell them what the topic will be. Then tell the students that those who didn't get a chance to speak today will get their chance the next time the group meets.

30. Is it all right to continue a Sharing Circle for an additional 10-20 minutes when we are doing a lot of sharing?

One result of an extended time limit may be an implied message: "I am going to continue the Sharing Circle until everyone shares," which is undesirable. There are other times, however, when the Sharing Circle has provoked such interest that the students want to continue the discussion. If time permits, continue, but officially end the session first. Twenty to thirty minutes is not magical, but we have found it is generally an appropriate period of time to carry out all the Sharing Circle procedures while most students remain actively attentive.

31. Since a Sharing Circle is an affective process, why do you have summary discussions at the end of every circle session?

The Sharing Circles is intended to be a confluent approach that prizes students' cognitive as well as affective development. The summary discussion satisfies the need of students to know what they learned from the activity. The cognitive aspects of Sharing Circles also help you justify the value of including an affective component in your curriculum, not only to your students but also to administrators, colleagues, and community. In addition to (or instead of) the summary questions listed in each Sharing Circle activity, you may create your own that relate your curriculum.

Additional Tips for Sharing Circle Leaders

Listen Actively

— Show external signs of listening through attentive posture, eye contact, nodding appropriately, smiling, gesturing, etc.

— Ask open-ended questions sparingly and only if they are non-threatening and facilitate the thoughts of the speaker: "Would you like to tell us more about that?"

— Ask specific questions to clarify what the speaker has said, or to help the speaker put into words what she or he wants to communicate—not to elicit more information.

— Allow time for silence and thought. Calm silence is trust-building. Don't feel you have to jump in every time someone stops talking.

— Watch for signals which may indicate that students want to talk. For example, students may lean forward, seek eye contact with you, steal glances at you, purse their lips, move their chairs closer, etc. Invite them to speak: "Do you have something to say, Jack?"

— Never take the "ball" away from the students. They are the stars.

— Accept all feelings as real without labeling them good or bad.

Give Recognition

— Look at each student gently and calmly when you speak to him or her.

— Use names when you address students in the circle.

— Thank each participant for his or her contribution. If participants are responding quickly and appropriately to each other, substitute nonverbal recognition: nods, eye contact, a smile.

— Praise good listening when another student is able to review or respond to what a speaker says: "You were listening."

Occasionally Facilitate a Review

— The purpose of the optional review is to give another increment of recognition to those students who spoke and those who listened attentively enough to review accurately.

— Be able yourself to repeat succinctly what each person has said. In the beginning, you will do most of the reviewing. If the student reviewing does not respond accurately to a particular individual, either ask that student or someone else to fill in or add to what was said in the review. This will ensure that all students in the circle feel they were listened to.

— Sometimes in a review, the students digress back to the topic. Don't "put down" someone who digresses, simply thank him and move on: "Thank you, Ed. Now let's see what we've talked about so far."

— Guide each reviewer to address the person to whom he is reviewing by name, rather than speak about her: "Sally, you said..." rather than, "Sally said..."

Focus on Similarities and Differences During the Discussion Phase

— Focusing on similarities and differences shows young people how much the same they are and that their differences are not a bad thing.

— The ability to verbalize similarities and differences implies a fairly advanced stage of development that we are not likely to find in very small children.

Involve Everyone

— To encourage the reticent young child, ask him if he would like to whisper his contribution to you or to someone next to him. When he whispers, respond encouragingly, then ask if he would like to tell the group also.

— Ask the reticent young child if the group could try to guess what her answer might be. Once she says okay, she becomes involved in saying yes or no, and usually shares eventually.

— Watch carefully for signs that reticent children want to be invited in. When you see such signs, ask gently: "Maria, would you like to take a turn?"

— Involve the timid by inviting them to review what someone just said. If they can get even one word out, you can give recognition for their good listening. They must go from tiny success to tiny success.

— Touch children who are "acting out" while giving eye contact to the person speaking. Have children change seats to separate troublesome pairs.

SHARING CIRCLE TOPICS

Fanciful and Fun

My Favorite Vacation

Introducing the Topic:

Our topic for today is, "My Favorite Vacation." By vacation, we are not referring to the school break you enjoy most, but to the specific trip or activity that has become your favorite among all the vacations you can remember. Maybe you went on an adventurous camping trip during one summer vacation, or perhaps you traveled by yourself to visit a grandparent, aunt, or friend. You may have participated in an intense summer training program where you perfected your skills in scouting, computers, swimming, or tennis. Maybe your family went skiing over the holidays, or perhaps you spent one holiday break working with an organization to provide shelter, food, and toys for the homeless. If your favorite vacation was spent right at home, reading and relaxing with family or friends, tell us about that. Paint a picture that will help us appreciate why you love the memory of this vacation so much. Think about it for a few moments. The topic is, "My Favorite Vacation."

Discussion Questions:

1. What makes a vacation memorable?
2. Why do people need to take vacations from school and work?
3. What would it be like to be on vacation all the time?

Life Skill Areas:

Self-Awareness, Relationships

A Secret Wish I Have

Introducing the Topic:

The topic for today's Sharing Circle is, "A Secret Wish I Have." We all play the wishing game at times. We wish for something and then we hope that our wish comes true. You've probably wished upon a star, over birthday candles, or at a wishing well or fountain. Wishing is fun. Tell us something that you've secretly wished for. Maybe you've wished for a dress, shirt, bike, game, or a trip to the Grand Canyon or Disney World. Perhaps you've wished for a European vacation or a particular kind of car. Secretly, you may wish that you had green eyes, or were taller or shorter. Or your wish may be for something like world peace and freedom from hunger for all people. Close your eyes for a moment and let your mind explore our topic, "A Secret Wish I Have."

Discussion Questions:

1. Why is wishing important?
2. What would life be like without wishes and dreams?
3. What are some things you can do to make wishes come true?

Life Skill Areas:

Self-Awareness, Goal Setting

Topic Variation:

"A Time I Wished for Something and My Wish Came True"
"A Time I Wished for Something and My Wish Didn't Come True"
"A Time I Helped Make Someone Else's Wish Come True"

What I Would Do If I Inherited One Million Dollars

Introducing the Topic:

The topic for today's Sharing Circle is, "What I Would Do If I Inherited One Million Dollars." Money can give you the option to do things that normally you could not do. Be creative as you imagine that you've just received news of a huge inheritance. What would you do? Would you go on a grand shopping spree for yourself and everyone you know? Would you fund research for AIDS or the environment? Would you start a business? What would you choose to do with one million dollars? Take a moment to think before you share with us on today's topic, "What I Would Do If I Inherited One Million Dollars."

Discussion Questions:

1. What feelings were common to our sharings?
2. How important is money in accomplishing good deeds?

Life Skill Areas:

Self-Awareness, Goal Setting, Decision Making

A Place Where I Feel Serene and at Peace

Introducing the Topic:

Today's topic is, "A Place Where I Feel Serene and at Peace." There are many types of places that contribute to our feeling serene and peaceful. Tell us about a place that creates these feelings in you. It could be a secluded spot, such as a wooded area or meadow, or maybe you'd sit beside a rushing river or placid lake. It could be a spacious room in your home, or a room that is small and cozy. Do you have a serene and peaceful view from your front porch or bedroom window? Do you love to sit in a favorite chair by the fireplace or on a bench in a busy park? Imagine feeling serene and peaceful and then tell us where you go to enjoy such feelings. The topic is, "A Place Where I Feel Serene and at Peace."

Discussion Questions:

1. What similarities and differences did you notice in the places that cause us to feel peaceful?
2. What characteristics about a place contribute most to your feelings of serenity and peace?
3. Under what circumstances could you feel serene in a very busy place?

Life Skill Areas:

Self-Esteem, Relationships, Stress Management, Self-Awareness

Someone I Would Like to Know Better

Introducing the Topic:

Today's Sharing Circle topic is, "Someone I Would Like to Know Better." We interact with many people every day. Some are friends. Others are acquaintances. Still others are strangers. Occasionally, we meet someone whom we wish we could know better. Has this ever happened to you?

Maybe the person you'd like to know better is a relative you see only occasionally at family gatherings. Maybe he or she is a classmate who sits across the room, or who shares only one class with you. Maybe the person you'd like to know is a celebrated athlete, actor, politician, or business executive. Or perhaps you simply want to spend time getting to know you grandparents better so that you can understand and appreciate all the things they've seen and accomplished in life. Think about it for a few moments. Our topic is, "Someone I Would Like to Know Better."

Discussion Questions:

1. What can you do to get to know someone better?
2. What obstacles can prevent us from getting to know new people?
3. What qualities in a person make you want to know him or her?

Life Skill Areas:

Relationships, Self-Awareness, Problem Solving

What I Think the World Needs To Be a Better Place

Introducing the Topic:

The Sharing Circle topic for today is, "What I Think the World Needs To Be a Better Place." How do you think the world could be improved? Would it be better if everyone had enough food to eat and had medical care? If people and countries talked to each other, would the world be improved? Would it be better if we all adopted the same environmental standards so that the world's air and water would be freer of pollution? Would you add more laughter and love and take away anger and hatred? Would you improve education and decrease weaponry? Think for a bit about all the things that could be done and describe the one you think most important. Today's topic is, "What I Think the World Needs To Be a Better Place."

Discussion Questions:

1. What would it take to actually realize the improvements we talked about?
2. What can *you* do to make the world a better place?

Life Skill Areas:

Self-Awareness, Problem Solving, Relationships

The Craziest Dream I Ever Had

Introducing the Topic:

Our circle session topic for today is, "The Craziest Dream I Ever Had." Dreams can help us to see things very differently from the way we see them when we're awake. Some dreams are so unlike the real world that they seem completely crazy.

We've all had crazy dreams. Sometimes those dreams give us clues to what is really going on inside of us, such as a strong wish or conflict. When the wish or conflict appears in a bizarre or otherwise disguised form, the dream seems crazy. Sometimes dreams provide inspiration for creative activities. Sometimes they help us solve problems. It is interesting to know that other people have crazy dreams, too. I invite you to share yours. If you do not have a dream to share, you might want to tell us about a fantasy or daydream. Our topic is, "The Craziest Dream I Ever Had."

Discussion Questions:

1. Why do people dream?
2. What purpose do dreams serve?

Life Skill Areas:

Communication, Self-Awareness

I Did Something Dreaming That I Couldn't Do Awake

Introducing the Topic:

Our topic for today is, "I Did Something Dreaming That I Couldn't Do Awake." Have you ever dreamed of doing something powerful, or heroic, or physically impossible, that you couldn't do in real life—like save the world, or fall off a high cliff and not get hurt? Maybe you've had a dream of flying, or lifting a skyscraper off the ground, or swimming across the ocean. If you would like to, tell us about your dream experience. The topic is, "I Did Something Dreaming That I Couldn't Do Awake."

Discussion Questions:

1. What parts of our dreams can we really do when we're awake?
2. What feelings do you have when you awake from a powerful dream?

Life Skill Areas:

Self-Awareness, Creativity

A Name I'd Like to Have

Introducing the Topic:

Today we're going to talk about, "A Name I'd Like to Have." Most people, at some point in their lives, wish they could change their name. One little girl named Cathy decided when she was two years old that her name was really Mary and, for almost a year, she answered only to that name. Other people have gone to court to change their names. What about you? Have you ever asked your parents why they decided to name you as they did? If you could choose your own name, what would it be and why? Let's talk about, "A Name I'd Like to Have."

Discussion Questions:

1. What similarities did you notice in the reasons we gave for picking our names?
2. Did the name you picked have to do with your real self, or did it go with some secret, fantasy self?
3. Why do you think names are so important to people?

Life Skill Areas:

Self-Awareness, Creativity

A Special Occasion or Holiday Related to My Culture That I Appreciate

Introducing the Topic:

In today's circle session, we're going to talk about something you've experienced that belongs to your culture. The topic is, "A Special Occasion or Holiday Related to My Culture That I Appreciate." Some special occasions are called "rites of passage." These are significant life events like the christening of a baby, a baptism, a bar or bat mitzvah, a wedding, or a funeral. They mark a person's passage from one stage in his or her life to another. Not every event of this nature is enjoyable, of course, especially if it marks the death of a loved one. But a funeral is still appreciated by many people because the ritual offers a kind of comfort.

Many of the values and attitudes handed down from one generation to another last a long time because they are a traditional part of a certain way of life; they stand for something treasured. Examples may be the Fourth of July for a citizen of the United States and Cinco de Mayo for Mexican-Americans. Other examples are holidays like Halloween, Easter, and Passover. Take a moment to think of a special occasion that relates to your culture—a rite of passage or a holiday that you particularly enjoy or appreciate. The topic is, "A Special Occasion or Holiday Related to My Culture That I Appreciate."

Discussion Questions:

1. What do holidays and special rites of passage do for people?
2. In what other ways are we influenced by out ancestors?
3. How do you feel about doing traditional things your ancestors did?

Life Skill Areas:

Values, Self-Awareness,

One Of My Favorite Possessions

Introducing the Topic:

Our topic for today is, "One of My Favorite Possessions." You probably own several things that are special to you. You may have had some of these possessions since you were very young, and you may have acquired others more recently. Tell us about one special thing you own, and describe what makes that item special. Someone you care for very much may have given it to you, or you may have done extra chores to earn enough money to buy it. It could be something that's fun to wear, or play with, or that looks nice in your room. Think about it for a moment. The topic is, "One of My Favorite Possessions."

Discussion Questions:

1. What is it that makes certain things special to us?
2. Do you think it's important for people to have favorite possessions? Why or Why not?

Life Skill Areas:

Self Awareness, Values

Topic Variation:

"Something I'd Like to Own."

The Funniest Thing That Ever Happened To Me

Introducing the Topic:

Today's topic is, "The Funniest Thing That Ever Happened to Me." We've all had many experiences in our lives that we think are funny. Tell us about the funniest one you can remember. Maybe you said or did something that cracked you up. Of perhaps it was someone else who did it, but you were involved. It could have been a pre-planned joke, or something that just happened spontaneously. Think about where you were and what was happening at the time. Take a moment and then share with us, "The Funniest That Ever Happened to Me."

Discussion Questions:

1. How does your body feel when you experience something really funny?
2. What are the benefits of having a sense of humor?

Life Skill Areas:

Self-Awareness, Creativity

My All-Time Favorite Movie

Introducing the Topic:

Today's topic is, "My All-Time Favorite Movie." This is a very enjoyable topic because it allows us to talk about something we really like. When it comes to movies, we all have our favorites. Some of us like adventure and mystery, others prefer romance and fantasy, still others like comedy. Think about the movies you have liked best, pick your very favorite, and tell us what it is and why you like it so much. The topic is, "My All-Time Favorite Movie."

Discussion Questions:

1. What are some similarities and differences in our preferences among movies?
2. If your feelings about a particular movie changed after listening to someone else talk about it, tell us which movie it was and what your thoughts are now.
3. What do we gain from movies? What do we learn?

Life Skill Areas:

Self Awareness, Values

Topic Variations:

This topic can be used with any favorite thing, such as a book, vacation spot, T.V. show, game, etc.

A Person I'd Like To Be Like

Introducing the Topic:

Our Sharing Circle topic today is, "A Person I'd Like To Be Like." Having role models is very important in life. People we admire are like a target to shoot for as we plan our future and live from day to day. Who is one of your role models? It could be a famous person you'd like to know, or maybe it's someone you *do* know, like a friend or family member. The person you want to emulate could be someone from history, or maybe even a fictional character. Think about what this person represents that makes you want to be like him or her. Take a few moments and, when you're ready to share, the topic is, "A Person I'd Like To Be Like."

Discussion Questions:

1. In what ways were our role models the same? ...different?
2. For those of you who know the person you'd like to be like, how do you feel when you're with that person? How does that person treat you?
3. Why is it important to admire people?
4. How do people we admire, whether we know them or not, teach us important lessons?

Life Skill Areas:

Self-Awareness, Relationships, Goals

My Idea of a Perfect Saturday Afternoon

Introducing the Topic:

Today's topic is a very enjoyable one. It is, "My Idea of a Perfect Saturday Afternoon." We all experience days that just seem to be perfect. Saturday is the day that many of us enjoy the most, probably because we don't have to be at school or work. If you could create an ideal Saturday afternoon, what would it be like? Think about where you would be, whom you would be with, and what you would do. Think of all the things that would make it a wonderful, special day. Then share your creation with us. The topic is, "My Idea of a Perfect Saturday Afternoon."

Discussion Questions:

1. Why didn't all of us create the same perfect Saturday afternoon?
2. What would life be like if every day were just as you described your perfect Saturday afternoon?

Life Skill Areas:

Self-Awareness, Values, Creativity

The Best News I Could Get Right Now

Introducing the Topic:

Today's topic is, "The Best News I Could Get Right Now." If you think about it for a moment or so, you can probably come up with a piece of news or information that, if you heard it this very minute, would make you feel really, really good. Maybe you entered a contest and are waiting to hear if you won, or perhaps you would like to hear from a close friend or relative. Your good news could be about you, or someone you know, or it could involve an important local, state, national, or world event. It might be earth-shattering news, or it might be something simple and personal. If someone walked through the door right now with a note for you, what would it say? The topic is, "The Best News I Could Get Right Now."

Discussion Questions:

1. What kinds of feelings do we experience when we get extremely good news? ...when we are waiting for news?
2. If I asked you to set a goal for yourself to help you receive the good news you want, what would your goal be?

Life Skill Areas:

Self-Awareness, Goals

Topic Variation:

"The Worst News I Could Get Right Now."

One of the Best Things That Ever Happened to Me

Introducing the Topic:

Our topic for this session is, "One of the Best Things That Ever Happened to Me." Take a moment to think about some of your most pleasant memories, and choose one to concentrate on. Your memory could be of something that happened recently or long ago.

Close your eyes and try to remember as much as you can about the event: the surroundings; the people involved; their words and actions; any special sounds, tastes, or smells; your feelings; and anything else that will make your memory more vivid. Spend a few moments reflecting. Then open your eyes and tell us about, "One of the Best Things That Ever Happened to Me."

Discussion Questions:

1. As you were sharing about your pleasant memory, did you experience the same emotions you felt when the event was actually happening? If so, where did those feelings come from?
2. How do we benefit be recalling and reliving our best memories?

Life Skill Areas:

Self-Awareness

Topic Variation:

"One of the Worst Things That Ever Happened to Me."

If I Had One Wish, It Would Be...

Introducing the Topic:

Our topic today is, "If I Had One Wish, It Would Be..." We all have dreams and wishes, things that may or may not come true but that bring us pleasure in the dreaming. Of all the wishes you have, pick one to share with us. It can be a big, grand wish like ending world hunger, or a simple wish like what you would like to have for your birthday. Take a moment to recall some of your wishes and dreams. The topic is, "If I Had One Wish, It Would Be..."

Discussion Questions:

1. Why do people wish for things?
2. What useful purpose is served by wishing?
3. What did you learn from this sharing circle about wishes and dreams?

Life Skill Areas:

Self-Awareness, Goal Setting

What I Would Do If I Were Made King or Queen of the World for One Day

Introducing the Topic:

Today we have a fun and fanciful topic. It is, "What I Would Do If I Were Made King or Queen of the World for One Day." Pretend that this could happen, and that you could do anything you wanted for one day. What would you do? Would you travel to a place you've never been before? Would you open Disneyland and Disneyworld to all the kids in the country? Would you have apartments built for all the homeless? Would you want to do something special for your family and friends, or for everyone in the world? Be creative! Be as wild and imaginative as you wish! When you are ready to share, the topic is, "What I Would Do If I Were Made King or Queen of the World for One Day."

Discussion Questions:

1. What are some of the similarities and differences you noticed in what we shared?
2. What kinds of a feelings would you experience in doing anything you wanted?

Life Skill Areas:

Self-Awareness, Responsibility, Creativity

Understanding Me

The Worst Trouble I Ever Got Into

Introducing the Topic:

Today's topic for the Sharing Circle is, "The Worst Trouble I Ever Got Into." Things sometimes happen that cause us to feel worried and concerned. When something we've done or a situation we're in threatens to produce a bad result (or *consequence*), we often say that we're "in trouble." There are many types of trouble to get into. Another person may be mad at us, we may find ourselves trapped in a difficult situation—we may even be in danger of physical harm. Take a few moments and think of the worst trouble you've ever been in and tell us about it. Maybe you were very late getting home, missed a deadline on a school project, went someplace you were not supposed to go, did something you were not supposed to do, got lost, or hurt yourself. Take a few moments and think about it. Our topic is, "The Worst Trouble I Ever Got Into."

Discussion Questions:

1. What were some of the feelings we had when we were in trouble?
2. What did you learn from the situation you described?
3. How can you avoid getting into trouble in the future?

Life Skill Areas:

Problem Solving, Communication, Self-Esteem

One Way I Wish I Could Be Different

Introducing the Topic:

Today's topic is, "One Way I Wish I Could Be Different." We all have things about ourselves that we'd like to change. Some of us wish we could change a physical feature or characteristic that we have no control over, like how tall or short we are. Others of us would like to make a change that would require a lot of effort and commitment, like a bad or annoying habit. What would you like to change about yourself?

Maybe you wish you were more patient, or smarter in math, or had red hair, or could dive from the high board without being afraid. You can share anything you'd like in this session, whether it's something you have lots of control over, or something you'll never really be able to change. The topic is, "One Way I Wish I Could Be Different."

Discussion Questions:

1. What did you learn or notice from our sharing and discussion on this topic?
2. Why are so few people satisfied with themselves just as they are?

Life Skill Areas:

Self-Awareness, Personal Mastery

Topic Variation:

"One Thing About Me I Never Want to Change"

A Secret Fear I Have

Introducing the Topic:

The topic of today's Sharing Circle is, "A Secret Fear I Have." A secret is something no one else knows about. Fear is an emotion that causes us distress, anxiety, or a sense of dread. All of us probably harbor secrets about ourselves, things we don't want anyone else to know. Perhaps we keep such things to ourselves because we think people won't like or accept us if they know; we are afraid they might laugh or make fun of us. Just as we all have secrets, we also have fears. Everyone is afraid of something. You may fear the dark, lightening and thunder, or strange dogs. You may have a fear of flying or being in high places. You may fear getting lost, being alone, swimming in deep water, or some other situation or thing. Think for a moment about a secret fear you have and are willing to share with us. Our topic is, "A Secret Fear I Have."

Discussion Questions:

1. What is something that we all have in common, based on what we shared?
2. How did it feel to share a secret? How do you feel now after taking that risk?
3. What have you learned about yourself from thinking or sharing on this topic?
4. What steps can we take to overcome our fears?

Life Skill Areas:

Self-Awareness, and Stress Management

Topic Variation:

"A Time I Was Afraid to Do Something But Did It Anyway"
"A Time I Helped Someone Who Was Afraid"
"A Time I was Scared and It Was Fun"
"A Way I Get Over Being Afraid"

A Significant Event in My Life

Introducing the Topic:

Today's topic is, "A Significant Event in My Life." There are many kinds of events that hold places of significance in our memories. What is one of the most significant that you can recall? It could be an achievement, such as winning an academic or athletic event or mastering a skill, or it could be a personal triumph, such as gaining control of a habit. Your significant event might be a move you made to new city or school. Or it might be a negative event, such as the death of a pet, or a divorce in the family. Think of one event in your life that you would like to share. Our topic is, "A Significant Event in My Life."

Discussion Questions:

1. How do negative events become significant in our lives?
2. Who decides how much significance an event has?
3. How do you think you will feel in five or ten years about events that are significant to you now?

Life Skill Areas:

Critical Thinking, Responsibility, Self-Esteem

Something I Want to Keep

Introducing the Topic:

Today in our Sharing Circle, we are going to talk about, "Something I Want to Keep." The term *keepsake* is usually applied to a material object of value to us, such as a souvenir or memento from a special event, a picture of a friend or loved one, or a gift received on a special occasion. Other things we like to keep are medals, plaques, and certificates of award. You might choose to keep the ball you used to make the winning point in an important game. Or your first doll, painting, or poem. You might also want to keep an intangible thing, such as your love of animals, or your respect for the environment. Choose one tangible or intangible thing that you want to keep and tell us why it is important to you. Our topic is, "Something I Want to Keep."

Discussion Questions:

1. What similarities did you notice in the things we want to keep?
2. What determines whether or not you decide to keep something?
3. How will you benefit by having your keepsake to look at ten or twenty-five years from now?

Life Skill Areas:

Self-Esteem, Decision Making, Values

Topic Variations:

"Something Tangible I Want to Keep"
"Something Intangible I Want to Keep"

One Question I Have About Life

Introducing the Topic:

Our topic today is, "One Question I Have About Life." Many questions arise in life. Some can be answered easily; others are not so simple. Sometimes we question why life isn't fair, or why there are wars, famine, illness, and injustice. We wonder why racism, sexism, and ageism exist, and why money is so important. Why mothers and fathers can't stay married, and where loved ones go when they die. We ask why people have to die at all, and why everything is always changing. Why some babies are born healthy and others not, and why some people think they have the right to make choices for everyone else.

What are you concerned about? Think of one question you have about life, and tell us what it is. We won't try to give you an answer, but we will listen and try to understand. The topic is, "One Question I Have About Life."

Discussion Questions:

1. Do you think there are workable answers to life's biggest questions? Explain.
2. If you had the authority, which of life's questions would you answer once and for all?
3. What did you learn from this topic?

Life Skill Areas:

Self-Awareness, Problem Solving, Decision Making

My Greatest Asset

Introducing the Topic:

Today's Sharing Circle topic is, "My Greatest Asset." Everyone has assets. In the financial world, our assets are property, stocks, cash—things that add to our wealth. Assets in our personal lives represent a different kind of wealth. They are the attributes we possess and the skills we've developed.

What is your greatest asset? Maybe it's your intelligence or your sense of humor. It might be your loyalty or your ability to make others feel comfortable, even in new situations. Maybe you are excellent at drawing, dancing, writing, computing, or growing things. Or perhaps you're good at listening, often hearing what others are feeling but not saying. Review some of the many assets you have, and choose the one you think is your greatest. Our topic is, "My Greatest Asset."

Discussion Questions:

1. Why is it important to recognize our assets?
2. Which are more important, personal assets or financial assets? Why?
3. Why is it sometimes difficult to talk about ourselves positively?

Life Skill Areas:

Self Esteem, Decision Making, Self-Awareness

Something I Need Help With

Introducing the Topic:

Our Sharing Circle topic for today is, "Something I Need Help With." It simply is not possible to be good at everything. There are times when all of us need some help. When do you?

Maybe you need help with a school subject, like math or French. You might need help learning to play the guitar or earning money. Perhaps you need help understanding adults or members of the opposite sex. Could you use some help starting an exercise program, or giving up junk food? Beginning a good habit or quitting a bad one? Everyone needs help with big things, and small things alike. Think about it for a moment, and tell us, "Something I Need Help With."

Discussion Questions:

1. What kinds of things do most of us seem to need help with?
2. What can you do to get the help you need?
3. Under what circumstances is "help" not very helpful?

Life Skill Areas:

Problem Solving, Relationships, Self-Esteem, Communication

Something About Me You Wouldn't Know Unless I Told You

Introducing the Topic:

Today's topic is, "Something About me You Wouldn't Know Unless I Told You." No one can figure out everything about us just by observing us or being around us at school. For example, unless we tell someone, no one will know about the great vacation I took over the summer, or the year you spent living in another country. So today, let's enlighten each other a bit. Let's tell each other about something we don't already know.

Maybe you work as a volunteer at a hospital or for a group like the Red Cross. Maybe you help out with young children at your church or synagogue. Perhaps you like to write poetry, paint, square dance, clog, or weave baskets. Or you might have won a talent contest at some time. Think about it for a few moments and see of you can come up with something that will surprise us. The topic is, "Something About Me You Wouldn't Know Unless I Told You."

Discussion Questions:

1. Why do you suppose we don't learn these things about each other outside the sharing circle?
2. How can we avoid judging people based on the obvious and the superficial?

Life Skill Areas:

Communication, Relationships, Self-Awareness

A Talent That I Possess

Introducing the Topic:

Today's Sharing Circle topic is, "A Talent That I Possess." Often we think of talented people as those who can write, draw, sing, dance or act. That is a narrow interpretation of talent. It also takes talent to build things, repair cars, and be a good listener. What is one of your talents? Perhaps you have a talent for understanding others, being a good friend, or settling disagreements. It takes talent to solve problems effectively, to entertain small children, and to teach others a new skill. Maybe you have a talent for making people laugh, or planning and organizing special events. Think of a talent that you have and tell us about it. Our topic is, "A Talent That I Possess."

Discussion Questions:

1. How does a person get talent?
2. Why are talented people sometimes referred to as "gifted?"
3. What can you do if you think you have a talent that no one else seems to recognize?

Life Skill Areas:

Self-Esteem, Self-Awareness

Something I Like to Do Alone

Introducing the Topic:

Our Sharing Circle topic today is, "Something I Like to Do Alone." Although most of us enjoy doing things with other people, there are some things we prefer to do alone. What is such a thing for you? Maybe you like to read or take walks alone. Perhaps you like to listen to music or study on your own. Sometimes it is fun to think or daydream in solitude. You might like to draw, write, or even dance alone. Some people love to sing, but wouldn't utter a note if other people were around. Think of one thing that you like to do alone and tell us how you feel when you are doing it. The topic is, "Something I Like to Do Alone."

Discussion Questions:

1. What are the advantages of doing some things alone?
2. How would some of the experiences we shared be different if they were done with others?

Life Skill Areas:

Self-Esteem, Self-Awareness

Two Things I Believe In That Conflict with Each Other

Introducing the Topic:

Today we are going to be talking about, "Two Things I Believe in That Conflict with Each Other." Very often we get trapped in a dilemma because we discover things about ourselves, or about our values, that don't fit together well. For example, I may be interested in saving gasoline because of the energy crisis, but when I'm late and in a hurry, I sometimes waste fuel by driving too fast.

Think about your own beliefs. Do they ever conflict? Maybe you believe in telling the truth, but occasionally lie because you also believe in protecting people from the truth if it might hurt them. And at what point does your loyalty to a friend become more important that your loyalty to rules or human rights? Have you ever been with good friends who asked you to do things you didn't want to do. When that happens, you have to decide what's more important, being with your friends or doing what you believe is right. Think about experiences like this that you have had. The topic is, "Two Things I Believe in That Conflict With Each Other."

Discussion Questions:

1. When two values conflict, how do you know which one is more important?
2. Is it necessary to resolve every value conflict that occurs within you?
3. What methods can you use to resolve your own conflicting beliefs?

Life Skill Areas:

Conflict Resolution, Self-Awareness

A Time I Stood Up for Something I Strongly Believe In

Introducing the Topic:

Today's topic is, "A Time I Stood Up for Something I Strongly Believe In." Most of us have experienced at least once the necessity to take a stand concerning something. Standing up for a belief can be difficult, especially if friends or relatives do not agree with us. Even when they do agree, it is not necessarily easy to state our beliefs publicly. Think of a time when this happened to you.

Maybe you saw others doing something that you felt was wrong, and you confronted them. Perhaps you were involved in a discussion about a controversial subject, and you stated your views, even though they were unpopular. You may remember being nervous and worrying about the uncertainty of the situation. Or you may have felt very sure of yourself. Perhaps when you look back on the occasion, you recall a sense of pride, accomplishment, or even daring. If the outcome was different from what you wanted, tell us what you learned from the experience. Remember, don't mention any names. The topic is, "A Time I Stood Up for Something I Strongly Believe In."

Discussion Questions:

1. What similarities were there in our reasons for standing up for what we believe in?
2. When is it hardest for you to stand up for your beliefs?
3. What conditions enable you to stand up for what you believe in?

Life Skill Areas:

Values, Self-Awareness, Assertiveness, Communication

Part of Me Wanted to Do One Thing, and Part of Me Wanted to Do Another

Introducing the Topic:

Our topic today is, "Part of Me Wanted to Do One Thing, and Part of Me Wanted to Do Another." Being torn between two choices is a common experience. Here's a typical example: One part of you—we'll call it the student part—wants to study and learn a subject well. Another part—the social part—wants to go to a party. Both parts are very real, but at times they are at odds with each other. Have you had a similar experience? Maybe you had a choice between going to a movie and going to a ball game, and part of you wanted the movie and part of you wanted the game. Or maybe you were torn between two equally tantalizing items on a lunch menu. Today let's talk about times when you were divided by a similar conflict. Take a minute and think about it. The topic is, "Part of Me Wanted to Do One Thing, and Part of Me Wanted to Do Another."

Discussion Questions:

1. What are the advantages of being a complex person with many different "parts?" What are some disadvantages?
2. How do you resolve an inner conflict like this when it occurs?

Life Skill Areas:

Self-Awareness, Conflict Resolution

I Said Yes When I Wanted to Say No

Introducing the Topic:

Today we are going to have a circle session about being assertive. We're going to talk about times when we found it tough to assert ourselves. The topic is, "I Said Yes When I Wanted to Say No."

Have you ever agreed to do something that you really didn't want to do? Maybe you agreed to attend a meeting that you really weren't interested in, or go to the park when you wanted to stay home. Or maybe someone asked to copy your homework and, instead of being assertive and saying no, you said okay. Take a moment to think about a time when something like this happened to you. The topic is, "I Said Yes When I Wanted to Say No."

Discussion Questions:

1. Why do you think people say yes when they really want to say no?
2. If you resent doing something you don't really want to do, but you agreed to do it, who's to blame?

Life Skill Areas:

Values, Peer Pressure, Self-Awareness, Communication

I Perceived Something Because It Was What I Wanted to Perceive

Introducing the Topic:

Today we are going talk about the topic, "I Perceived Something Because It Was What I Wanted to Perceive." Often we enter into situations with certain expectations. We think something "should" happen and so we see or hear it even if it isn't there. This is a *perception*, but it is an *incorrect* perception. Can you think of a time when you saw or heard something, not because it was really there, but because it was what you wanted to see or hear?

Maybe you wanted your team to score a run so badly that you "saw" a teammate slide into home safely, while everyone else saw the play as an out. Or maybe you "heard" your parent say that you could spend the night with a friend, but later found out that no such permission was given. If you would like to share, tell us about a time when your perception played this type of trick on you. The topic is, "I Perceived Something Because It Was What I Wanted to Perceive."

Discussion Questions:

1. Why do you think people see the things they want to see, and hear the things they want to hear?
2. How can you avoid making errors in perception like these?

Life Skill Areas:

Awareness, Communication

An Experience I Had That Caused Me to See Things Differently

Introducing the Topic:

Today our topic is, "An Experience I Had That Caused Me to See Things Differently." Sometimes, a very special kind of experience causes us to shift our point of view and see things in a different way. An experience like this is sometimes called a *turning point*.

For example, maybe someone you didn't like very well unexpectedly did you a favor and, all of a sudden, you saw that person in a completely new light. Or perhaps a world event that affected a lot of people made you think of your own life in a different way. You might have read something in a book or seen something in a movie that affected you very strongly, or maybe you were moved by the words to a song. Whatever it was, if you would like to share, tell us about, "An Experience I Had That Caused Me to See Things Differently."

Discussion Questions:

1. Did you notice any similarities in the kinds of experiences we had that caused us to see things differently?
2. How did you develop your original perception—the one that changed?
3. Which perception is correct—the old one or the new one? How can you be sure?

Life Skill Areas:

Awareness, Values, Responsibility

When I Felt Comfortable Just Being Me

Introducing the Topic:

Our topic today is, "When I Felt Comfortable Just Being Me." Think about a time when you really felt comfortable with a person or group. Perhaps you could do or say anything you wanted, and you felt the other person or group would understand and accept you. Try to recall a time when you were not being one bit phony—you were being very real, or genuine.

What was the other person's (or the group's) attitude and how did he or she behave toward you? Was the person accepting? ...welcoming? ...uninterested? ...talkative? ...relaxed? ...critical? ...happy? ...bored? Think about it for a minute, and tell us what about the person and the situation made you feel like being yourself. The topic is, "When I Felt Comfortable Just Being Me."

Discussion Questions:

1. What are some attitudes and behaviors in others that allow us to feel comfortable and act genuinely?
2. How do you feel inside when you are being genuine? When you are being phony?
3. How do you feel toward another person when he or she is being genuine? ...phony?

Life Skill Areas:

Self-Esteem, Mastery, Communication

Something I Hate To Do

Introducing the Topic:

We all occasionally find ourselves doing something that we don't like to do. Today, we're going to have an opportunity to talk about times like that. Our topic is, "Something I Hate To Do."

What is one of your *least* favorite things to do? Maybe it's something you have to do on a regular basis, like clean your room, mow the lawn, or take a test. Or perhaps it's something that only happens once in a while, like writing a term paper or giving a speech. I'm sure you can think of many things you don't like doing, but pick just one to share with us. The topic is, "Something I Hate To Do."

Discussion Questions:

1. What similarities did you notice in the things we hate to do?
2. When you're doing something you dislike, do you think your attitude affects how well you perform?

Life Skill Areas:

Self-Awareness, Responsibility

Topic Variation:

A good topic to proceed or follow this one is:
"Something I Love To Do."

Something I Like About Myself Right Now

Introducing the Topic:

Today's Sharing Circle topic is, "Something I Like About Myself Right Now." You could respond in many ways to this topic. Maybe you like some physical part of you, like your hair or the freckles on your nose. Perhaps what you like is that you are studying hard and doing well in a particular subject. Maybe you like the way you recently handled a tough problem, or how you are relating to a friend.

Really think about this for a minute, and identify something that is currently giving you a good feeling about yourself. If you decide to share, tell us what you like about yourself and how it makes you feel inside. Our topic is, "Something I Like About Myself Right Now."

Discussion Questions:

1. Is it easy or difficult to talk about yourself in a positive way? Explain.
2. Why is it important to have positive feelings about yourself?
3. How can you expand your positive beliefs about yourself to other areas?

Life Skill Areas:

Self-Awareness, Self-Esteem

Topic Variation:

"Something I Dislike About Myself Right Now."

One Thing I Am Sure I Can Do Well

Introducing the Topic:

In today's circle, we will be focusing on things we are good at. Our topic is, "One Thing I Am Sure I Can Do Well." Notice that with this topic you are asked to brag a little, and that's okay. You are not boasting and you are not comparing yourself to anyone else. Neither are you putting anyone down. You are simply describing what you *know* you can do.

Think about one thing that you do well. It could be something you do at school or it could take place away from school. You may have done it once, or many times. Think about it for a minute and, if you will, share with us on the topic, "One Thing I Am Sure I Can Do Well."

Discussion Questions:

1. When did you realize that you could do this thing well? How did you get to that point?
2. Why is it important to feel that we can do some things well?
3. Tell us something you learned about a person in the circle that you didn't know before.

Life Skill Areas:

Self-Awareness, Self-Esteem, Personal Mastery

I Did Something That Made Me Feel Like a Good Person

Introducing the Topic:

Our Sharing Circle topic today is, "I Did Something That Made Me Feel Like a Good Person." We do many things that cause us to feel good about ourselves. Sometimes we do them spontaneously (on the spur of the moment) and sometimes we plan them in advance. Tell us about something you did that resulted in positive feelings. You may have done it for yourself, or for another person—or perhaps it was for an animal or the environment. Other people may have known about what you did, or you may have kept it to yourself until now. Think about it for a few moments. The topic is, "I Did Something That Made Me Feel Like a Good Person."

Discussion Questions:

1. When we feel we have done something good, is it important to get recognition from someone else? Why or why not?
2. How can you encourage yourself to do more good things so that your positive feelings will spread to other parts of your life?

Life Skill Areas:

Self-Awareness, Self-Esteem, Relationships, Responsibility

Why I Sometimes Like To Be Alone

Introducing the Topic:

Today, our discussion topic is, "Why I Sometimes Like To Be Alone." People like to be alone for many different reasons. Some people like to be alone to experience peace or harmony with nature, or just to think over a problem. Others like to be alone to escape or get away from something, like noise, people, or work. Think about the reasons you've had for wanting to be alone, and tell us about the one that stands out in your mind as perhaps the most important. In addition, if you decide to share, describe the feelings you have when you are alone. The topic is, "Why I Sometimes Like To Be Alone."

Discussion Questions:

1. What are some similarities and differences in our reasons for wanting to be alone?
2. How can being alone help us get to know ourselves better?

Life Skill Areas:

Self-Awareness, Relationships

Topic Variation:

A good topic to precede or follow this one is:
"Why I Sometimes Like To Be With Others"

Feelings

How I Feel About War

Introducing the Topic:

Today's topic is, "How I Feel About War." Feelings are facts. Feelings are not right or wrong, they just *are*. Your feelings are uniquely your own and, at the same time, they may be similar to the feelings of others. Sometimes your feelings are mixed. You feel good and bad about the same thing. Today we're going to describe our feelings about war. We have not experienced a war in this country for a long time. However, we have participated in armed conflicts in other parts of the world. An example of such a conflict is the Gulf War. How do you feel about war? Do you feel good, bad, glad, sad, scared, or angry? Perhaps you have more than one feeling when you think about war. Take a few moments to get in touch with your feelings. The topic is, "How I Feel About War."

Discussion Questions:

1. What similarities did you notice in the feelings that were shared?
2. How do you suppose you developed your feelings about war?
3. What can you do to influence your country's actions with respect to peace and war?

Life Skill Areas:

Self-Awareness, Conflict Resolution, Decision Making

Topic Variations

"How I Feel About the Homeless"
"How I Feel About the Environment"
"How I Feel About Discrimination"
"How I Feel About Drugs"
"How I Feel About World Hunger"

This is a very powerful forum for any number of variations. You may tie into a particular classroom learning theme, an event that involves your students, or some unsettling news in the media. It is very important not to judge feelings as they are shared. The purpose of this circle is to get students in touch with their feelings, not to edit or alter them.

How I React When I'm Angry

Introducing the Topic:

Our topic today is, "How I React When I'm Angry." Everybody gets angry. When we get angry, we all have some sort of reaction. Some of us shout, some of us stuff our anger deep inside us, some of us lash out and hit other people or things, and some of us throw and break things. How do you behave when you're angry? Maybe you dive into an activity of some kind and try to keep busy. Perhaps you're one of the many people who handle anger by withdrawing and becoming very silent. Or maybe you react verbally, saying things that you regret later. Think about this for a moment and, if you would like to share, the topic is, "How I React When I'm Angry."

Discussion Questions:

1. What did you learn about handling anger from this Sharing Circle topic?
2. What do you think are the most effective ways of handling anger?
3. What purpose, if any, does getting angry serve?

Life Skill Areas:

Problem Solving, Decision Making, Communication, Relationships

Topic Variations:

"How I React When I'm Excited"
"How I React When I'm Happy"
"How I React When I'm Sad"

Something I Did That Helped Someone Feel Good

Introducing the Topic:

Our topic today is, "Something I Did That Helped Someone Feel Good." We are all affected in some way by the behavior of others toward us. And we have the ability to influence how others feel. Think of a time when you deliberately did something that you knew would trigger a positive reaction in someone. Perhaps your friend was having a bad day and you said something funny that made him or her laugh. Perhaps you did an extra chore at home to help a family member who was feeling overworked. Think of the many things you have done because you wanted someone else to feel good, and share one example with us. Our topic is, "Something I Did That Helped Someone Feel Good."

Discussion Questions:

1. How do *you* feel when you do something nice for someone else?
2. How do you *benefit* by doing something helpful for another person?
3. When we feel good about ourselves and when we help others, how are we affecting the world we live in?

Life Skill Areas:

Self-Awareness, Conflict Resolution, Team Building, Friendship

Topic Variations:

"Something I Did That Made Someone Feel Bad"
"I Did Something To Make Someone Feel Good But He/She Got Mad Instead"

A Time I Disappointed Someone

Introducing the Topic:

Our topic today is, "A Time I Disappointed Someone." Different people expect different things from us. Sometimes we know we are going to disappoint someone and it cannot be avoided. Sometimes we don't want to, hope we won't, and do anyhow. There are lots of ways to disappoint someone. Think of an example from your life. Your parent might have expected you to complete a task and you didn't. A friend might have expected you to go to the movies and you couldn't. Sometimes you might even disappoint yourself! You might have expected to get an A on a book report you wrote, and then discovered that you got only a C. Maybe you told a small lie and got caught. Close your eyes and think for a moment of a time when you heard those words, "I'm disappointed in you." When you're ready, our topic for sharing is, "A Time I Disappointed Someone."

Discussion Questions:

1. How do you feel when you disappoint someone?
2. What is the relationship between expectation and disappointment?
3. What can you do about someone's disappointment in you?

Life Skill Areas:

Stress Management, Decision Making, Responsibility

Topic Variations:

"A Time Someone Disappointed Me"
"Something I Find Disappointing"

A Time I Couldn't Control My Curiosity

Introducing the Topic:

Our topic today is, "A Time I Couldn't Control My Curiosity." Curiosity is a wonderful emotion that can add excitement to our lives and motivate us to learn new things about ourselves and our world. However, sometimes we are expected to control our curiosity, and that can be difficult. Tell us about a time when you lost control of your curiosity.

Maybe you peeked inside a gift that was not supposed to be opened until Christmas or your birthday. Perhaps you couldn't wait to find out what happened in a story, so you looked at the last page. Have you ever been walking down a hall and looked in a room to see what was going on, or glanced through someone's window at night, even though what was happening inside was none of your business? Have you ever tried to hear what some people next to you were saying, just because their conversation sounded interesting? Take a few moments to think of a time when you gave in to your curiosity. The topic is, "A Time I Couldn't Control My Curiosity."

Discussion Questions:

1. How do you feel when you have to fight to control your curiosity?
2. Why do you think we have this emotion? What does curiosity do for us?

Life Skills Areas:

Self-Awareness, Creativity

It Made Me Feel Good to Make Someone Else Feel Good

Introducing the Topic:

The topic today is, "It Made Me Feel Good to Make Someone Else Feel Good." When we contribute to good feelings in others, we usually feel good ourselves. In fact, we sometimes benefit as much as the recipient. Think of a time when you enjoyed positive feelings by making someone else feel good.

Maybe you helped a new student find a classroom, or went out of your way to compliment someone's appearance. Perhaps you helped someone understand a difficult math concept, or taught a new player how to pitch a curve ball. You may have stood up for someone who was being bullied or teased. Or you may have helped an elderly neighbor carry groceries. Tell us about one time when you helped another person feel good and in the process felt good yourself. The topic is, "It Made Me Feel Good to Make Someone Else Feel Good."

Discussion Questions:

1. Why do we feel good when we help someone else feel good?
2. What sort of planning is required to make someone feel good?
3. What would this school be like if we all spent a little more time helping others feel good?

Life Skill Areas:

Relationships, Communication, Responsibility

Topic Variation:

"Something Someone Did for Me That Made Me Feel Good"
"Something I Did for Someone Else That Made Him/Her Feel Good"

How Somebody Hurt My Feelings

Introducing the Topic:

Today we are going to talk about, "How Somebody Hurt My Feelings." Our feelings get hurt in many ways. Frequently, we feel hurt because of something that someone else did. The person who hurt us may not even realize the effects of his or her actions. Can you think of a time when someone hurt you?

Maybe a friend didn't invite you to a party or ignored you when you wanted to talk. Perhaps someone called you a name, or said something rude to you. Maybe a coach cut you from a team, or a teacher reprimanded you harshly in front of other students. Choose a time when your feelings were hurt. Tell us what happened and how you felt, but please don't mention any names. The topic is, "How Somebody Hurt My Feelings."

Discussion Questions:

1. What kinds of things tend to hurt our feelings most?
2. What are some ways we can cope with hurt feelings?
3. What role do our expectations play in whether or not we feel hurt?

Life Skill Areas:

Relationships, Self-Esteem, Coping Skills

How I Feel When People Tell Me They Like Me

Introducing the Topic:

Today's Sharing Circle topic is, "How I Feel When People Tell Me They Like Me." Usually when someone tells us they like us, we feel pleased, but this kind of compliment can generate other feelings as well. For example, we might feel uncomfortable, or embarrassed, or obligated in some way to respond.

How do you feel when people are openly admiring of you? Maybe you feel powerful or more lovable. You might feel pleased, happy, or warm all over. Maybe you feel like you have to tell the person that you like him or her, too. If that's the case, you may feel uncomfortable, even a bit resentful. Think about a time when someone told you he or she liked you, and tell us how you felt. Our topic is, "How I Feel When People Tell Me They Like Me."

Discussion Questions:

1. What would you think about a person who didn't seem to care whether he or she was liked or not?
2. Why do positive remarks and compliments sometimes cause us to feel uncomfortable?
3. Do you have to like everyone who likes you? Why or why not?

Life Skill Areas:

Relationships, Communication, Self-Esteem

Something In My Life I Am Happy About

Introducing the Topic:

Today's topic is, "Something in My Life I Am Happy About." When good things happen in our lives, we are not only grateful for them, we feel happy as well. What are some things you are happy about in your life? Maybe you have wonderful relationships with family and friends. You might be happy about earning good grades, or having unusual athletic ability or musical talent. Perhaps you are happy about your excellent health, intelligence, or sense of humor; or your artistic creativity, leadership ability, or computer skills. Review some of the things in your life that you are happy about and share one. The topic is, "Something In My Life I Am Happy About."

Discussion Questions:

1. Based on the things we shared, what's your reaction to the popular saying, "Money doesn't buy happiness."?
2. What are some things that contribute greatly to happiness that we tend to take for granted?
3. Who decides what makes you happy?

Life Skill Areas:

Self-Awareness, Self-Esteem

Topic Variation:

"Something In My Life I Am Proud Of"

A Time I Got My Feelings Hurt

Introducing the Topic:

Today's Sharing Circle topic is, "A Time I Got My Feelings Hurt." All of us have had our feelings hurt. The only way to avoid it is to bury our feelings where no one can touch them, and that's never a good idea.

Tell us about a time when your feelings were hurt. Maybe you wanted to play in a game and the coach wouldn't let you. Perhaps you were unjustly accused of doing something and you were hurt because your accuser didn't believe you. Have you ever learned that a friend had been talking about you behind your back? Have you ever been hurt because someone didn't trust you, or because a sister or brother got to do something you didn't? Describe what happened and how you handled your hurt feelings. The topic is, "A Time I Got My Feelings Hurt."

Discussion Questions:

1. Do you think hurt feelings are caused more by our perception of an event or by the event itself? Why?
2. Why do our feelings get hurt in some situations and not in others?

Life Skill Areas:

Self-Awareness, Self-Esteem, Relationships

I Could Have Hurt Someone's Feelings, But I Didn't

Introducing the Topic:

Today our topic is, "I Could Have Hurt Someone's Feelings, But I Didn't." We have all been in situations where we could have said or done something to hurt another person. This sort of opportunity presents itself frequently, for a variety of reasons. Think about a time when you were in this position. Maybe someone said or did something that wasn't appropriate, and you could easily have corrected or criticized the person, but for some reason you decided against it. Perhaps you heard someone exaggerate or lie in order to impress people, but you decided not to let on that you knew the truth. Or when someone made an embarrassing mistake, perhaps you bit your tongue and didn't laugh. Your decision might have been based on friendship, or fear that the person might hurt you back, or your realization that what the person was going through at that moment wasn't easy. Think about an experience you've had like this and, without telling us who the person was, share what happened. Our topic is, "I Could Have Hurt Someone's Feelings, But I Didn't."

Discussion Questions:

1. What were some of the things that kept us from hurting other people's feelings?
2. How did you feel about yourself for making the choice not to hurt someone's feelings?
3. What was the most important thing you learned in this session?

Life Skill Areas:

Self-Awareness, Personal Mastery, Relationships

A Time When I Trusted Myself

Introducing the Topic:

Our discussion topic today is, "A Time When I Trusted Myself." There are a lot of times in our lives when we really need to ask someone for help or advice. But there are other times when we have to trust our own judgment and experience. Think of a time when you trusted yourself. Maybe you had to make a decision, and even though you couldn't predict what would happen, you knew that no one else could either. It was up to you. Or perhaps you were struggling with a problem for which only you knew the solution. You may have felt nervous or afraid, but you pushed ahead anyway and tried your solution. Maybe someone asked you a tough question and you decided to trust the first answer that popped into you mind, even though you weren't sure it was correct. Take a minute and think of a time when you trusted your own knowledge and experience. Our topic is, "A Time When I Trusted Myself."

Discussion Questions:

1. What similarities did you notice in the things we shared during this session?
2. What prevents you from trusting yourself more often to handle situations effectively?
3. How can you learn to trust yourself more?

Life Skill Areas:

Self-Awareness, Self-Esteem, Personal Mastery

When Someone Criticized Me

Introducing the Topic:

In this session, we are going to focus on the effects of criticism. The topic is, "When Someone Criticized Me."

Think about a time when someone criticized you, and try to remember how you felt when it happened. Recall the situation and what was going on that brought about the criticism. Perhaps you felt the criticism was unjust or too harsh, or simply not helpful. Or maybe you think that if the situation had been reversed, you would have criticized the other person for doing the same thing. Maybe you gained some new insight or understanding from the criticism. Do you think the criticism accomplished what it was intended to accomplish? Did you profit, or did you suffer, or both? Take a minute to think about it. The topic is, "When Someone Criticized Me."

Discussion Questions:

1. Are there some ways of offering criticism that are more effective than others? What are they?
2. When is criticism positive, and when is it negative?
3. What is meant by the term, "constructive criticism?"

Life Skill Areas:

Self-Esteem, Awareness, Communication, Conflict Resolution

A Time I Felt Totally Alive and in Touch With the World

Introducing the Topic:

Our topic today is, "A Time I Felt Totally Alive and in Touch With the World." Think of, and try to re-experience, a time when you felt that almost every aspect of your life was coming together perfectly. A moment when your physical, mental, emotional, and spiritual sides seemed balanced and you felt truly at home on the planet. This sort of moment is often called a "peak experience."

Perhaps you were in a special place and feeling full of joy and energy. Maybe your feelings were influenced by the person or people you were with. Or maybe you had just reached a goal toward which you had been working for some time. Think back over the years and try to recall such a moment. Our topic is, "A Time I Felt Totally Alive and in Touch With the World."

Discussion Questions:

1. Why do peak moments like these occur so rarely in the lives of most people?
2. What are the ingredients of a peak experience and how can we create more wonderful moments like these?

Life Skill Areas:

Awareness, Personal Mastery, Self-Esteem

A Feeling of Sadness I Remember

Introducing the Topic:

Our topic for this session is, "A Feeling of Sadness I Remember." We all feel sad at times. Life regularly presents us with its negative as well as its positive side.

Can you remember a time when you felt sadness or grief about something? Maybe you lost a relative, a friend, or a pet. Perhaps you saw a homeless person and were struck by the sadness of his or her plight. Or maybe you were moved to sadness by the impact of a movie, a play, or a piece of music. Let's observe a minute of silence and think of times we've experienced sadness. If you decide to share, the topic is, "A Feeling of Sadness I Remember."

Discussion Questions:

1. What lessons, if any, do sad experiences offer us?
2. Is it wise to try to avoid all sad experiences? Why or why not?
3. What is the relationship between sadness and love?

Life Skill Areas:

Self-Awareness

A Time I Was Alone, But Not Lonely

Introducing the Topic:

Our topic for this session is, "A Time I Was Alone, But Not Lonely." Being alone and feeling lonely are not the same thing. Sometimes it's nice to get away and be by oneself. Alone times give us an opportunity to relax, reflect, and plan. We are less distracted and less influenced by others when we are alone. We can get to know and understand ourselves better.

Try to remember a time when you were alone and felt good about it. Tell us where you were, what you were doing, and how you gained from the experience. The topic is, "A Time I Was Alone, But Not Lonely."

Discussion Questions:

1. What is the difference between being alone and being lonely?
2. Are people ultimately alone with their feelings? ...their thoughts? Why or why not?
3. How might a person turn loneliness into a positive experience?

Life Skill Areas:

Self-Awareness, Personal Mastery, Relationships

A Feeling I Had a Hard Time Accepting

Introducing the Topic:

Today our Sharing Circle topic is, "A Feeling I Had a Hard Time Accepting." Some feelings can be difficult or even painful to accept. When we are experiencing them, we'd give anything to make them go away. Later, we wish we could erase them from memory. Jealousy, for example, is a very uncomfortable feeling that at times leads to destructive and violent behavior. Guilt is a feeling that eats away inside and sometimes leads to self-punishment.

Tell us about a time when you experienced a feeling that you didn't want to have to deal with. Maybe you were afraid of something, angry with someone, disgusted by an unpleasant incident, sad over a loss, or filled with loneliness. Take a few moments to think about it. The topic is, "A Feeling I Had a Hard Time Accepting."

Discussion Questions:

1. What similarities and differences did you notice in the feelings we talked about and our reactions to them?
2. Have you ever made a feeling go away and, if so, how?
3. What advantages are there to accepting and experiencing negative feelings?

Life Skill Areas:

Self-Awareness, Personal Mastery

A Favorite Feeling

Introducing the Topic:

Our topic for this session is, "A Favorite Feeling." Some feelings are such a reward in themselves that we welcome them. Think about it. Perhaps a favorite feeling for you is the happiness, joy, or elation you experience when you engage in a particular activity, like running, hiking, surfing, or dancing. Or maybe one of your very favorite feelings is the pride you experience when you finish a task or reach a goal. Maybe you particularly enjoy the feeling of peace or inspiration you experience when you are on a mountain top or in a magnificent building. Your favorite feeling might be amusement, excitement, relaxation, power, or love.

Feelings are often best described by their effects on us, so feel free to tell us what your favorite feeling does to your skin, stomach, heart, head, and other parts of your body. Tell us too, about a specific time you experienced this feeling. Our topic is, "A Favorite Feeling."

Discussion Questions:

1. What were some similarities in the reactions these feelings produced in our bodies?
2. Under what circumstances do feelings like the ones we have been discussing recur? Can we deliberately do things to get them back?

Life Skill Areas:

Self-Awareness, Responsibility

A Thought I Have That Makes Me Feel Happy

Introducing the Topic:

Today we are going to talk about, "A Thought I Have That Makes Me Feel Happy." Has it ever occurred to you that what you think about can affect how you feel? When you think sad or angry thoughts, do you start feeling depressed? And when you have positive, uplifting, happy thoughts, don't you begin to feel that way, too. Our thinking really does make us feel certain emotions. In this sharing circle, I want you to *think* about something that gives you a happy feeling. Your thoughts might focus on a fun time, or a good friend, or a treasured pet. You might think about your favorite food, or joke, or leisure activity. You can choose any thought, as long as the feeling that follows it is happy. The topic is, "A Thought I Have That Makes Me Feel Happy."

Discussion Questions:

1. What did you learn from this session about how our thoughts affect us?
2. How can we have control over our thoughts?
3. If positive thoughts make you feel better, why do you bother having negative thoughts at all?

Life Skill Areas:

Self-Awareness, Personal Mastery

Topic Variation:

"A Thought I Have That Makes Me Feel Unhappy"

Relationships

A Time I Said "No" to Peer Pressure

Introducing the Topic:

The topic for today's Sharing Circle is, "A Time I Said 'No' to Peer Pressure." We all want to be liked and accepted by others. Even though differences are what make us unique, we often wish we could be just like everyone else. Sometimes we say and do things we don't *really* agree with, just so others will like and accept us. If everyone else is doing something, it's not easy to be different. Think of a time when, in spite of your desire to be one of the group, you had the courage to say "no." Maybe you said "no" to excluding a classmate from an activity, or perhaps you said "no" to cheating on a test, smoking a cigarette, using a drug, or drinking alcohol. Take a few moments to think about it. Our topic is, "A Time I Said 'No' to Peer Pressure."

Discussion Questions:

1. How comfortable are we in expressing our true feelings and opinions with one another?
2. What are some ways we can learn to say "no?"
3. How will developing the ability to say "no" help you become a happier, more successful person?

Life Skill Areas:

Relationships, Self-Esteem, Assertiveness, Decision Making

Topic Variation:

"A Time I Wanted to Say 'No,' But Didn't"

Things I Do To Keep a Friend

Introducing the Topic:

Our Sharing Circle topic for today is, "Things I Do to Keep a Friend." A friend is someone about whom we have special feelings. For all of us, having friends is important. So is keeping them. We all have special ways of expressing our friendship, such as making time for a friend, talking with and listening to a friend, and giving thoughtful gifts or cards. What do you do to keep a friend? Maybe you simply tell your friend how much you value his or her friendship. You may go places or do things that your friend enjoys, even when you'd rather be doing something else. Close your eyes for a moment and think of the many things you do to keep a friend. When you're ready we'll begin sharing. Our topic is, "The Things I Do to Keep a Friend."

Discussion Questions:

1. Why is it important to work at keeping friendships alive?
2. How do your friends feel about the things you do?
3. What would happen if you didn't do anything to keep your friendships going?

Life Skill Areas:

Communication, Self-Awareness, Relationships, Friendship, Self-Esteem

Topic Variation:

"Something I Never Do When I Want to Make Friends with Someone"
"One of the Nicest Things a Friend Ever Did for Me"

Someone Showed Me That He or She Liked Me

Introducing the Topic:

Today's topic is, "Someone Showed Me That He or She Liked Me." People don't always come right out and tell us that they like us. Sometimes they demonstrate it with the things they do. Can you think of a time when you knew someone liked you, not through words, but through actions? Maybe this person included you in an activity, or invited you to team up on a class assignment. Perhaps the person gave you a compliment, or offered to help you with a difficult task. Or maybe the person supported you when you were in some kind of trouble. People show they like us in many different ways. Think about it for a moment. Our topic is, "Someone Showed Me That He or She Liked Me."

Discussion Questions:

1. Which is a more reliable indicator of how a person feels, words or actions? Why?
2. Which is easier for *you*, telling people that you like them or doing things to show you like them? Explain.
3. What do you conclude when a person who says he or she likes you, does things that indicate otherwise?

Life Skill Areas:

Relationships, Communication, Self-Esteem

Topic Variation:

"I Showed Someone That I Liked Him or Her"

A Time I Was the Leader of a Group

Introducing the Topic:

Our topic today is, "A Time I Was the Leader of a Group." All of us belong to various groups—project groups at school, friends with whom we spend time, clubs to which we belong. Groups often form for specific activities, and then dissolve. While they exist, most groups have one or more leaders. Think of a time when you took the lead in a group. Maybe you were chosen to chair a committee, or volunteered to be a project leader in class. Perhaps you organized a group to play basketball or baseball, or led a group of friends to a secret hideaway, or found yourself in charge of all the neighbor kids on Halloween night. All of us have taken the lead many times in many different activities. Think of one example and tell us about it. The topic is, "A Time I Was the Leader of a Group."

Discussion Questions:

1. How did you feel when you were a leader?
2. What did it take to become the leader in the situation you described?
3. Why do groups need leaders?

Life Skill Areas:

Relationships, Communication, Personal Mastery

One Way I Changed to Be a Better Friend

Introducing the Topic:

The topic for today's Sharing Circle is, "One Way I Changed to Be a Better Friend." For one reason or another, we've all lost friends. We may have moved away—or perhaps they did. Or we may have done something that actually destroyed the friendship. We've all made mistakes in our friendships and maybe we've learned how to be a better friend in the process.

If you've had this type of experience, tell us how it changed you. Maybe you don't take your friends for granted anymore, or gossip about them behind their backs. Maybe you try not to be jealous when they spend time with other people. Possibly you found out that it's not a good idea to date the ex-boyfriend or ex-girlfriend of a friend. Or maybe the change involves being more honest with your friends, and keeping quiet about the things they tell you in confidence. Think about it for a few moments. The topic is, "One Way I Changed to Be a Better Friend.

Discussion Questions:

1. What qualities seem to be essential in a good friend?
2. How difficult was it to bring about the change you described?
3. What value is there in discussing a topic like this one?

Life Skill Areas:

Relationships, Self-Esteem, Communication, Friendships

Topic Variation:

"How I Lost a Friend"

A Way I Will Always Depend on People

Introducing the Topic:

Our topic today is, "A Way I Will Always Depend on People."
Unless we become hermits, most of us will always depend on
other people. We need to be loved and to have friends. We want
to talk and share with others. We socialize with people, and ask
their help in making choices. We work for people who pay us, go
to school with people who help us learn, and choose a life partner
for mutual support.

Consider some of the ways that you depend on people now.
Which of those ways satisfies a need that you think will always
be there, no matter how successful and independent you become.
Think about it for a few moments and, if you choose to share, tell
us, "A Way I Will Always Depend on People."

Discussion Questions:

1. What similarities and differences did you notice in the ways we
   depend on people?
2. What are the benefits of depending on others? What are the
   drawbacks?
3. Does anyone live a totally isolated, independent existence?

Life Skill Areas:

Relationships, Self-Esteem, Values

People Seem to Respect Me When...

Introduction to Topic:

Our Sharing Circle topic today is, "People Seem to Respect Me When...." To respect a person is to admire and hold that person in high regard or esteem. When do people seem to respect you? Is it when you tell the truth or follow through on what you say you will do? Perhaps people seem to respect you when you get good grades or demonstrate the ability to solve problems. Perhaps you notice the respect of others when you employ a good strategy to win a game, or come home on time, or complete your homework regularly. Standing by your convictions, even though they are unpopular, and your ability to say no when appropriate will always inspire respect. Take a few moments to think of something you do that people respect. Our topic is, "People Seem to Respect Me When...."

Discussion Questions:

1. Why is it important to earn the respect of others?
2. How can you tell whether someone respects you?
3. What are some things that can lead to a loss of respect on the part of others?

Life Skill Areas:

Self-Awareness, Self-Esteem, Relationships, Responsibility

Something I Like to Do With Other People

Introducing the Topic:

Today's topic is, "Something I Like to Do With Other People." It's fun to do things with other people. Most games require two or more people, as do many sports, such as football, baseball, even tennis. Think of something you like to do with other people. It might be shopping or talking on the phone. Perhaps you like big family picnics or holiday dinners. Or maybe you enjoy having lunch with friends. Do you have more fun at amusement parks when you are with a group? Think of one thing you like to do with other people and tell us about it. The topic is, "Something I Like to Do With Other People."

Discussion Questions:

1. What do we gain by experiencing events and activities with other people?
2. What happens when a group gets too large for a particular activity? What are the effects of having too few people?

Life Skill Areas:

Self-Awareness, Relationship, Communication

I Was Nice to Someone Because He or She Made a Good First Impression

Introducing the Topic:

Today we are going to discuss the topic, "I Was Nice to Someone Because He or She Made a Good First Impression." Have you ever noticed how first impressions affect us? We look at people and for some reason we like them right away, just because of the way they look—or we have just the opposite reaction.

Can you remember a time when you saw someone and were very nice to that person for no reason other than the fact that s/he made a good first impression on you? Perhaps you welcomed this person into some kind of group you were involved in, or smiled at him or her in class. Or maybe you offered to help when you saw that the person needed assistance. If you would like to share, tell us about a time when something like this happened to you. The topic is, "I Was Nice to Someone Because He or She Made a Good First Impression."

Discussion Questions:

1. Who really creates a first impression, the "impressor" or the "impressee?"
2. How do circumstances and the environment affect first impressions?
3. How can you improve or control the first impression *you* make?

Life Skill Areas:

Communication, Self-Awareness, Friendship, Relationships

A Group I Like Belonging To

Introducing the Topic:

Today our topic is, "A Group I Like Belonging To." One of the most important things in life for most of us is being part of a group of people whom we enjoy and with whom we share common interests or goals. So today we are going to talk about groups we belong to and how it feels to belong.

If you decide to share, tell about a group you belong to. It could be a club or organization here at school, at church, or somewhere else. Or it could be a group of friends that gets together frequently. Tell about one thing the group does that you enjoy, how you contribute to it, what the group contributes to you, and how you feel about belonging. Today's topic is, "A Group I Like Belonging To."

Discussion Questions:

1. Why do people join groups, clubs, and organizations?
2. Why are some people "loners" who don't associate with groups?
3. How can a group give the impression that it is open to new members?

Life Skill Areas:

Friendship, Values, Relationships, Communication

A Time I Didn't Want to Be a Member of a Group

Introducing the Topic:

Today's topic is, "A Time I Didn't Want to Be a Member of a Group." When it comes to belonging or not belonging to a group, we usually do have a choice. There may be times when we'd rather not be included.

Think about a time when you avoided getting involved with a group or left a group after you were already a member. Was your decision influenced by the way you were feeling that day, by other things you had to do, or was there something about the group you didn't like? Perhaps the group was going to do something you did not want to do, or expressed values or beliefs contrary to your own. Without naming the group or telling us who was in it, describe the situation and your feelings at the time. The topic is, "A Time I Didn't Want to Be a Member of a Group."

Discussion Questions:

1. What were the main reasons we shared for not wanting to be included in a group?
2. Who decides what groups you belong to? How are those decisions made?
3. What can you do if a group to which you *do* belong starts engaging in activities you don't agree with?

Life Skill Areas:

Values, Relationships, Decision Making, Assertiveness

A Way I Show I'm a Good Friend

Introducing the Topic:

Our topic for this session is, "A Way I Show I'm a Good Friend."
There are many things we can do to demonstrate that we are a
good friend. We can be helpful and supportive *all* the time, and
we can do special things on special occasions. How do you show
your friendship? Maybe you show it in the way you handle
disagreements, or offer to help when your friend is in a jam.
Maybe it's something as simple as being a good listener. Think
about the things you do for your friends. When you're ready to
share, the topic is, "A Way I Show I'm a Good Friend."

Discussion Questions:

1. What are some similarities and differences in the ways we show
   we're a good friend?
2. Why is it important to actively show that you're a good friend?
3. How do you feel when you are being a good friend?

Life Skill Areas:

Relationships, Self-Awareness, Communication, Friendship

What I Value Most in a Friend

Introducing the Topic:

Good friends can be and do many things for each other. I would like you to decide what some of those things are for today's circle topic, "What I Value Most in a Friend."

What do you and your friends say and do to make your friendships work, and to make them special? What qualities do you think are important in a friend? Do you value honesty? ...loyalty? ...listening? ...common interests? ...having time to be together? Think about it for a moment and, when you are ready, our topic is, "What I Value Most in a Friend."

Discussion Questions:

1. What are some of the main qualities that we value in friends?
2. How do you feel about your friend when he or she does or says something that you think is valuable to the friendship?
3. If you want your friends to behave in the ways we talked about, would be wise for you to do the same things? Why?

Life Skill Areas:

Relationships, Self-Awareness, Communication, Friendship

Something I Appreciate About My Parent(s)

Introducing the Topic:

The topic for our Sharing Circle today is, "Something I Appreciate About My Parent(s)." Parents are the people who take care of us. They may be the parents we were born to, or adopted by, or they may have come to us through a second marriage. When someone else cares for us, such as a foster parent, grandparent or other relative, that person is *like* a parent. Today we're going to think about positive things that we value about our parents. You may talk about one parent, or both. Perhaps you appreciate your parents for listening when you talk about your feelings or activities. Maybe your parents show their trust in you by allowing you to make many decisions for yourself, or maybe you appreciate the guidelines they have set for you. Do you have a parent with a great sense of humor? Does your parent help out at school or with a team or organization you belong to? Take a few moments and pick something you especially appreciate about one or both of your parents. Our topic is, "Something That I Appreciate About My Parent(s)."

Discussion Questions:

1. What kinds of feelings did you experience as you were sharing about your parent or parents?
2. How can we express the positive things we feel about our parents?
3. If you choose parenthood in the future, how can knowing what you appreciate in your own parents help you do a better job of parenting?

Life Skill Areas:

Communication, Support Systems, Relationships

Topic Variations:

"Something About My Parent(s) I Wish I Could Change"
"A Time My Parent(s) Really Made Me Feel Special"
"If I Were a Parent, I'd..."

A Rule We Have In My Family

Introducing the Topic:

The Sharing Circle topic for today is, "A Rule We Have In My Family." Families like all other organizations have to establish rules. You are probably glad to have some family rules, but don't feel so good about others. Think about the rules in your family and describe one to us.

Maybe your family has a rule that requires you to finish your chores before playing or going out with friends. Maybe homework must be completed before watching television, and no name-calling or fighting is allowed. Some families have rules about bedtime, having friends over when no adult is home, and maintaining a degree of cleanliness and order in each person's room. Think about the rules in your family and choose one to share. Our topic is, "A Rule We Have In My Family."

Discussion Questions:

1. How well do the rules work in your family?
2. How would things be different if your family did not have these rules?
3. If you have a family, what rules do you think you will establish?

Life Skill Areas:

Relationships, Problem Solving, Communication

Topic Variation:

"One Rule I Wish Our Family Didn't Have"
"A Rule I Think Our Family Needs"

Somebody Whose Opinion I Value Very Much

Introducing the Topic:

Today's Sharing Circle topic is, "Somebody Whose Opinion I Value Very Much." This topic gives us a chance to talk about someone we admire and whose opinions we respect. This could be someone you know personally, such as an older brother or sister, a friend, or a neighbor whom you look up to and are able to talk with. Or it could be someone you don't know personally but whose opinions you respect, like a T.V. personality, a movie star, or a politician. Think about it for a minute and, if you will, tell us a little about one person who's opinion you value. The topic is, "Somebody Whose Opinion I Value Very Much."

Discussion Questions:

1. Did you notice any similar characteristics in the people whose opinions we value?
2. How are you like the person whose opinion you value?
3. Why is it important to choose people to look up to and respect?

Life Skill Areas:

Relationships, Values, Self-Awareness

An Important Person in My Life

Introducing the Topic:

Our Sharing Circle topic today is, "An Important Person in My Life." Most of us interact with many people every day. Some are friends, some are relatives, and some are strangers. The people who are important to us have usually contributed something special to our lives. For example, they may look after us, guide us, or teach us. Frequently they share our joys and sorrows.

Tell us about one important person in your life. This person could be a parent, grandparent, teacher, counselor, or coach. He or she could also be a friend. Tell us how and why this person is important to you, and how you feel when you are with him or her. Our topic is, "An Important Person in My Life."

Discussion Questions:

1. What characteristics did our important people have in common?
2. If your important person were no longer available to you, how would you manage to get along?

Life Skill Areas:

Relationships, Self-Awareness

A Promise That Was Hard to Keep

Introducing the Topics:

Today, our topic is, "A Promise That Was Hard To Keep." Notice that this is a topic that allows you to go either way. You can talk about how you kept your promise, or you can talk about a promise that proved too difficult to keep.

When we make a promise, we are pledging our word. But sometimes we agree to something that, although it may not have seemed overwhelming at first, proves very difficult in the long run. Other times, we know right from the start that it will be tough, but for some reason we promise anyway. Think of a promise that you found hard to keep and tell us the circumstances, the outcome, and your feelings along the way. Please remember not to use names. The topic is, "A Promise That Was Hard to Keep."

Discussion Questions:

1. How do you feel about yourself when you are able to keep a promise? ...able to keep a promise?
2. How are promises related to honesty, integrity, and trust?
3. What did you learn from this topic that you would like to mention?

Life Skill Areas:

Relationships, Responsibility, Self-Awareness

Someone Tried to Make Me Do Something I Didn't Want to Do

Introducing the Topic:

Today's topic has long been a favorite of students in the circle because it has happened to so many of them. The topic today is, "Someone Tried to Make Me Do Something I Didn't Want to Do." Maybe you can think of a time when someone you knew—perhaps a friend or a group of friends—wanted you to go some place or do something against your better judgment. Maybe you thought it might be harmful to you or someone else, or maybe it was illegal.

The thing to focus on here is how you handled the situation. Did you go along with the person? If you did, how did you feel about it later? If you decided not to go along, how did you feel about that? Did it have any effect on your relationship with the person? This sort of situation can be very tough to handle; when it happens, we feel put on the spot. If you decide to share your experience, tell us what happened and how you felt, but don't tell us who was pressuring you. The topic today is, "Someone Tried to Make Me Do Something I Didn't Want to Do."

Discussion Questions:

1. What makes situations like this seem like no-win situations?
2. Which matters more—doing what you believe is right or shielding other people from disappointment?
3. Have you observed or learned anything of interest to you in this session that you would like to mention?

Life Skill Areas:

Peer Pressure, Values, Relationships, Assertiveness

Someone Did Something for Me
That I Appreciated

Introducing the Topic:

Today's circle session topic is, "Someone Did Something for Me That I Appreciated." Have you ever had someone do something for you that you thought was out of the ordinary, or unexpected, or particularly nice? Tell us about it.

The person could have been a member of your family, a teacher, or a friend. Maybe a brother or sister offered to help you with a difficult task, or a friend brought you a book to read when you were home with the flu. Perhaps you received an unexpected birthday greeting, or a phone call from someone who wanted to wish you good luck in a big game. Think for a moment about something like this that's happened to you. If you let the person know how you felt, tell us about that, too. The topic for today is, "Someone Did Something for Me That I Appreciated."

Discussion Questions:

1. Did you notice any similarities in the things we shared?
2. What are some other ways that people influence each other's feelings?

Life Skill Areas:

Self-Awareness, Relationships

Someone Was Phony With Me

Introducing the Topic:

Our topic today is, "Someone Was Phony With Me." Think about a specific time when you sensed that someone was being phony with you—a time when you were trying to interact with a person who was hiding behind a "mask." The incident could have happened at school, in a store, at home—just about anywhere. It could have occurred a long time ago, or very recently.

How did you know the behavior was phony? How did you react? Were you able to accomplish anything with this person, or did the phoniness create too strong a barrier? Think about it for a moment and, when you share, please don't mention names. The topic is, "Someone Was Phony With Me."

Discussion Questions:

1. When one person in a group is being phony, what effects does the behavior have on the rest of the group?
2. Why do you think people pretend to be something or someone they're not?
3. When someone is being phony, how can you make contact with the real person behind the facade?

Life Skill Areas:

Relationships, Communication

I Felt Good Enough About Myself to Reach Out to Someone Else

Introducing the Topic:

Today's topic is, "I Felt Good Enough About Myself to Reach Out to Someone Else." Think about how your feelings about yourself influence the way you relate to other people. Can you remember a time when you felt discouraged or depressed? Or perhaps you were at a party, feeling scared or shy for some reason. Was it hard for you to reach out to others?

Now think of a time you really felt good about yourself. Maybe you had recently accomplished a big project, or had just finished exercising, or were wearing a new outfit. Because of the way you felt about yourself, you reached out and made contact with someone else. Think about it for a minute, and tell us what happened. The topic is, "I Felt Good Enough About Myself to Reach Out to Someone Else."

Discussion Questions:

1. Why do our feelings about ourselves have such a strong influence on our ability to relate to others?
2. Why do some people always seem to have difficulty reaching out to others?
3. When you are feeling shy, what can you do about it?

Life Skill Areas:

Self-Esteem, Friendship

After I Got to Know Someone, I Liked Him or Her, Even Though I Didn't At First

Introducing the Topic:

Have you ever met someone you didn't particularly like at first and found out later that he or she was really nice? Our topic for today deals with how this happens. It is, "After I Got to Know Someone, I Liked Him or Her, Even Though I Didn't at First."

Think of a time you experienced this kind of turnaround. The person may have been male or female, and your first meeting may have occurred recently or a long time ago. It could have been at school, in your neighborhood, or just about anywhere else. Without mentioning names, tell us about your first impressions of this person, and then describe how you felt about the person after you got to know him or her. Think about it for a minute. The topic is, "After I Got to Know Someone I Liked Him or Her, Even Though I Didn't at First."

Discussion Questions:

1. Why are first impressions often unreliable?
2. What can you do to avoid making snap judgments based on first impressions?

Life Skill Areas:

Friendship, Communication

Someone Who Trusts Me

Introducing the Topic:

Our topic for this session is, "Someone Who Trusts Me." All of us experience many feelings in our lives. Some are good feelings, and some are bad. Sometimes, we tend to take the good feelings for granted; we fail to appreciate them, or even forget about them completely. An example is the good feeling we have when someone trusts us.

Think of someone who trusts you, and how that trust makes you feel. This is someone who feels good enough about you and what you are capable of doing that he or she believes in you whole-heartedly. This is probably someone who likes to have you around, and who doesn't find it necessary to question or check up on you very much. This "someone" could be a parent, friend, relative, teacher—even an pet. Take a minute to think about it, and then let's discuss, "Someone Who Trusts Me."

Discussion Questions:

1. Do you find that you usually trust people who trust you? Why or why not?
2. Why do you think the person you talked about trusts you?
3. What kinds of qualities and behaviors tend to earn the trust of others?

Life Skill Areas:

Relationships, Trust, Self-Esteem

School

The School Rule I Think Is Most Important

Introducing the Topic:

The topic for today's Sharing Circle is, "The School Rule I Think Is Most Important." All schools have rules. Sometimes we think that these rules just get in the way, but imagine what might happen if we didn't have them. In deciding what you think the most important school rule is, consider the benefits each rule offers. You might be happy there is a "listen when others speak" rule because you are quiet and shy and wouldn't be heard without such a rule. Maybe you appreciate a rule against hitting other people and damaging property. Or perhaps you think the most important rule is the one that prohibits tobacco, alcohol, and other drug use. Think about the school rules and tell us which one you think is the most important. The topic for today is, "The School Rule I Think Is Most Important."

Discussion Questions:

1. Which rules do we seem to think most important?
2. Who is responsible for establishing classroom rules? ...school rules?
3. What would happen if there were no rules?

Life Skill Areas:

Problem Solving, Responsibility

Topic Variation:

"A School Rule I Would Like to Add"
"A School Rule I Would Like to Change"
"A School Rule I Would Like to Eliminate"

I Do My Best in School When...

Introducing the Topic:

Today's Sharing Circle topic is, "I Do My Best in School When...."
School is not always the easiest place to be, and performing well
in school can be a real challenge. We all do better in some
situations than in others. And we all have certain conditions we
prefer. What does it take for you to do your best in school?

Do you perform best when your teacher seems to respect you and
expect a lot of you? Do you find it necessary to like a teacher in
order to do well in a class? Maybe you do your best in school
when things are going well at home, or in your peer relationships.
Or perhaps you have found that it helps to set specific goals in
your classes. Consider the circumstances under which you do
your best in school, and tell us about one. The topic is, "I Do My
Best in School When...."

Discussion Questions:

1. What seems to be our biggest motivator for doing well in school?
2. How can you use the insights you've gained from today's circle?

Life Skill Areas:

Self-Awareness, Self-Esteem, Problem Solving

How I Feel About Homework

Introducing the Topic:

The topic for today is "How I Feel About Homework." Homework is a requirement in most of your classes. Doing homework can reinforce what you learn in the classroom and can provide you with new information. What are your feelings about homework? Do you feel good about doing it? Do you hate it and think it's a waste of time? Tune into yourself and tell us why you feel as you do. The topic is, "How I Feel About Homework."

Discussion Questions:

1. What is the value in feeling good about what you do?
2. How do your feelings influence what you get out of a homework session?
3. What are your thoughts about homework? How are your feelings affected by your thoughts?

Life Skill Areas:

Self-Awareness, Responsibility

Topic Variations:

"A Time Doing Homework Really Helped Me"
"The Best 'I Don't Have My Homework Done' Excuse I Ever Used"

What I Like Most About This School

Introducing the Topic:

Our topic for today's circle is, "What I Like Most About This School." There is hardly anything that is all good or all bad and that includes school. So today, I'd like you to think about what you like best here at this school. Maybe there's a teacher you really like, or a course that you find particularly interesting. Maybe what you like best is getting to see your friends every day, or playing sports or participating in other extracurricular activities. Think about it for a few moments, and decide what about this school gives you positive feelings. The topic is, "What I Like Most About This School."

Discussion Questions:

1. In what ways is a topic like this important to students? ...to teachers?
2. When there is one thing that you really like about school, how does that feeling affect your attitude toward the rest of school?

Life Skill Areas:

Self-Awareness, Decision Making, Responsibility

Topic Variation:

"What I Like Least About This School"

For more variations to the topic, "What I Like Most About...," add "This Town," "This Country," "This Holiday," "This Season of the Year," etc.

A Change I Would Make to Improve This School

Introducing the Topic:

We all know that nothing is perfect; there is room for improvement in almost every aspect of life. For today's topic, I'd like you to think about things you would like to see improved here at school. The topic is, "A Change I Would Make to Improve This School."

School is something you are involved in on a daily basis, so you can probably think of a number of changes you would like to make. Your improvement might involve classes, the school building, extracurricular activities, the schedule, breaks, anything at all. If you could make one recommendation, what would it be? Think about it. When you are ready to share, the topic is, "A Change I Would Make to Improve This School."

Discussion Questions:

1. What were some similarities and differences in our ideas for improving this school?
2. What does it take to make change in an institution like a school?

Life Skill Areas:

Self-Awareness, Responsibility

How I Learn Best

Introducing the Topic:

In this Sharing Circle, we're going to talk about, "How I Learn Best." We all have certain things we do that help ourselves learn. What are your most effective ways of learning? Do you like to work by yourself, or do you prefer to discuss the material you are studying with someone else? Do you learn best by reading information, or do you need to hear it or write it down? Some people learn best when they are involved in a project that allows them to build something. We all have different methods of learning things. Take a few moments to think about *your* favorite methods. The topic is, "How I Learn Best."

Discussion Questions:

1. Why do we differ in the ways we learn best?
2. How does it help us to be aware of the ways we learn best?
3. What could this school do to make learning easier for you?

Life Skill Areas:

Self-Awareness, Goal Setting, Personal Mastery

Topic Variation:

"Something That Hinders My Learning"

Communication

What I Think Good Communication Is

Introducing the Topic:

Today's topic for discussion is, "What I Think Good Communication Is." Communication is an exchange of thoughts, feelings, opinions, or information between two or more people. Today we're going to focus on the ingredients of good communication. There are no right or wrong answers; whatever you contribute will help us develop a better understanding of what's involved. If you like, try thinking about a person with whom you've communicated successfully and attempt to isolate some of the things that happen during your interactions with that person. Take a few minutes, and then we'll begin sharing on our topic, "What I Think Good Communication Is."

Discussion Questions:

1. What quality or ingredient of good communication was mentioned most often during our sharing?
2. Why is it important to practice good communication?

Life Skill Areas:

Communication, Self-Awareness

Topic Variation:

"What I Think Poor Communication Is"

Someone Pointed Out Something Good About Me

Introducing the Topic:

Today's topic is, "Someone Pointed Out Something Good About Me." When you hear someone describe something nice about you, you probably feel very good. However, if you have a difficult time accepting compliments, that good feeling may be mingled with a bit of discomfort. Think of a time when someone—a friend, relative, neighbor, or teacher—pointed out something good about you! Maybe this person stated that you were considerate, responsible, attractive, industrious, or smart. The statement may have been made directly to you, or to someone else who then shared it with you. Recall the situation, what the person said, and how you felt. The topic is, "Someone Pointed Out Something Good About Me."

Discussion Questions:

1. How did most of us react when we were told something good about ourselves?
2. How do you handle any discomfort you feel when receiving compliments?
3. Why is it important to share our positive thoughts about people?

Life Skill Areas:

Communication, Relationships

When What Was Said Was Not What Was Meant

Introducing the Topic:

Today's topic is, "When What Was Said Was Not What Was Meant." I am sure if you think about it, you can remember a time when a person you know said one thing and meant something entirely different. Perhaps a friend said it was okay for you to go to the movies on a night that he or she couldn't go, and later got mad because you did. Or someone expressed liking for your new haircut and later criticized the haircut behind your back. Have teammates or classmates ever gone along with an idea you suggested and then fought it every step of the way? Think for a moment about a time this happened to you, and describe how you handled the situation. When you're ready, we'll begin sharing on the topic, "When What Was Said Was Not What Was Meant."

Discussion Questions:

1. How important is it to say what you mean? Why?
2. Why do people say things they don't mean?
3. If you think someone's words are insincere, what can you do?

Life Skill Areas:

Communication, Values, Relationships

A Time When I Accepted Someone Else's Feelings

Introducing the Topic:

As we all know, it means a lot to each of us to have our feelings accepted. When someone accepts your feelings, it is the same as accepting you. In this session we are going to turn this idea around and talk about how it feels to be the acceptance *giver*. The topic is, "A Time When I Accepted Someone Else's Feelings."

Can you remember a time when you gave your attention to someone and accepted his or her feelings? Maybe you listened carefully to a friend who was angry with you for breaking a promise. Or you may have accepted your parent's frustration about the condition of your room. Perhaps you listened to a teammate who accused you of playing unfairly or uncooperatively. Keep in mind that the most difficult feelings to accept are those that are different from your own, yet true acceptance means listening without getting angry, defensive, or judgmental. Think about it for a few moments. The topic is, "A Time When I Accepted Someone Else's Feelings."

Discussion Questions:

1. When is it hardest to accept someone else's feelings?
2. How can you discipline yourself to listen and accept negative feelings when they are directed at you?
3. What is gained by accepting the feelings of others?

Life Skill Areas:

Friendship, Communication, Relationships

A Time When It Was Okay to Express My Feelings

Introducing the Topic:

Our topic today is, "A Time When It Was Okay to Express My Feelings." In our circle sessions, we talk about our experiences and how those experiences affect our feelings. In fact, this is a place where we are all encouraged to share our feelings. This is not true of all situations. There are some places where stating one's feelings is neither appropriate nor wise.

Tell us about a time, outside the circle, when it was okay for you to express your feelings. Tell us, too, how you felt experiencing that kind of freedom and acceptance. Maybe something happened at home and your parent made a point of asking how you felt about it. Of maybe you expressed your feelings to a friend, without being invited, because you knew they would be accepted. Have you ever expressed your feelings in class, knowing it would be okay? Think about it for a moment. The topic is, "A Time When It Was Okay to Express My Feelings."

Discussion Questions:

1. How are people affected when their feelings are not accepted?
2. Why do people sometimes keep their feelings to themselves when they would receive greater acceptance and respect if they expressed them?
3. How can you determine if it's okay to express your feelings?

Life Skill Areas:

Communication, Relationships, Assertiveness

Once When Someone Wouldn't Listen to Me

Introducing the Topic:

Today we are going to talk about one of the frustrations that occurs in the communication process. The topic is, "Once When Someone Wouldn't Listen to Me."

Have you ever tried to get someone listen to you, and failed? Tell us about it. Maybe you came home wanting to relate an exciting experience to your family and no one would stop long enough to listen. Perhaps you had a question while shopping, but the salesperson ignored you. Or maybe you were dealing with a particularly troubling problem and tried to discuss it with a friend, but he or she kept changing the subject or getting distracted. Take a minute to think about it, and tell us about a time when you had an experience like this. The topic is, "Once When Someone Wouldn't Listen to Me."

Discussion Questions:

1. What similarities and differences did you notice in our feelings about not being listened to?
2. How can you handle situations in which you aren't being listened to?
3. What have you learned from this discussion about listening to others?

Life Skill Areas:

Relationships, Communication

How I Get People to Pay Attention to Me

Introducing the Topic:

Today our topic is, "How I Get People to Pay Attention to Me." When you or I want to communicate with someone, first of all we have to get that person to focus on us. There are many ways to do this. For example, if you do something funny, destructive, or bizarre, people will automatically look at you. If you don't want every head in the room to turn, you have to do something less unusual. What do *you* do?

How do you get the attention of a family member engrossed in a T.V. program? What do you do to get the attention of a friend some distance from you in a large crowd? How do you capture the attention of someone two tables away in a quiet classroom or library? If you can think of a specific incident in which you used a particular method, tell us about it. The topic is, "How I Get People to Pay Attention to Me."

Discussion Questions:

1. When do we need to capture the attention of others?
2. What relationship is there between the *way* you get attention, the *kind* of attention you get, and *how long* the attention lasts?
3. How do you feel when a person refuses to pay attention to you no matter what you do?

Life Skill Areas:

Self-Awareness, Relationships, Communication, Assertiveness

A Time When Listening Would Have Kept Me Out Of Trouble

Today's topic is, "A Time When Listening Would Have Kept Me Out Of Trouble." This session offers us the chance to learn something about ourselves and the value of listening.

Can you remember a time when someone told you not to do something, maybe even explained why you shouldn't, and you didn't listen and ended up in trouble? Have you ever failed to listen when a teacher gave instructions concerning how to complete a school assignment and, therefore, completed it incorrectly? These are examples of times when listening would have paid off. I'm sure you can think of others. Take a moment before you share on our topic, "A Time When Listening Would Have Kept Me Out Of Trouble"

Discussion Questions:
1. How important is it to be a good listener?
2. What can you do to become a better listener?

Life Skill Areas:
Communication, Self-Awareness

Topic Variation:
"A Time I Listened Well"

I Told Someone How I Was Feeling

Introducing the Topic:

Our topic today is, "I Told Someone How I Was Feeling." Have you ever come right out and told someone how you were feeling about him or her? Think of a time you were very open in this way. Perhaps you were feeling joyful or amused at something the person did and you wanted him or her to know it. Perhaps you expressed strong negative feelings, like anger or resentment, in response to something the person did.

How did the person react? Was he or she pleased, respectful, surprised, angry, or defensive? What happened as a result of your openness? Think it over for a minute, and tell us about a time you were forthright in expressing your feelings. The topic is, "I Told Someone How I Was Feeling."

Discussion Questions:

1. Why do we sometimes hesitate to tell others our feelings?
2. When is it generally a good idea to tell people how you feel? When is it generally not a good idea?

Life Skill Areas:

Self-Awareness, Communication, Assertiveness, Relationships

A Time I Listened Well to Someone

Introducing the Topic:

Most of us appreciate having someone really listen to us. In this session we are going to turn this idea around and talk about how it feels to listen to someone else. The topic is, "A Time I Listened Well to Someone."

Can you remember a time when you really paid attention to someone and listened carefully to what he or she said? This means that you didn't interrupt with your own ideas or daydream about your own plans, but really concentrated and tried to understand what the other person was attempting to get across. Maybe you've listened to a friend like that, or a younger brother or sister, or a teacher or coach. Think about it for a few moments and, if you wish, tell us about, "A Time I Listened Well to Someone."

Discussion Questions:

1. What kinds of things make listening difficult?
2. Why is it important to listen to others?
3. What could you do to improve your listening?
4. How do you feel when someone really listens to you?

Life Skill Areas:

Self-Awareness, Personal Mastery, Relationships

Topic Variation:

Other related topics that help students understand the importance and profound affects of listening are:

"A Time I Failed to Listen to Someone"
"A Time Someone Really Listened to Me"
"A Time Someone Failed to Listen to Me"

Something I See Differently Than My Parents' Generation Sees It

Introducing the Topic:

Today our topic is, "Something I See Differently Than My Parents' Generation Sees It." People's opinions are influenced by their perceptions and their perceptions are influenced by their opinions. It is very natural for people of different generations to see things differently.

You probably have some views that are similar to those of your parents' generation. And you probably see some issues very differently. Do you think that your views differ on music, or the need for military spending, or the importance of a college education? Do you think the older generation has a different view of environmental problems, health care, or work? Tell us about one difference as you perceive it. If you don't think there are any significant differences, tell us how you came to that conclusion. The topic is, "Something I See Differently Than My Parents' Generation Sees It."

Discussion Questions:

1. Just for a minute, imagine that you are a member of your parents' generation and grew up in the same conditions and circumstances as they did. How do you think you would see some of the issues that were brought up in this session?
2. Knowing your parents, how do you think they would react if they were growing up in the conditions and circumstances that make up your world?

Life Skill Areas:

Values, Self-Awareness, Communication

How I Used Sharing Circle Skills Outside the Circle

Introducing the Topic:

By now you have participated in several circle sessions, and you've had a chance to practice the positive communication skills that are used in the circle. The purpose of this session is to give you an opportunity to talk about other situations in which you've had an opportunity to use some of those same skills. The topic is, "A Time I Used Sharing Circle Skills Outside the Circle." Think about it for a moment.

Can you remember a time when you used a circle skill in some other setting? Maybe you listened very well, or spoke clearly, or were conscious of the need to share time equally with other people who wanted to talk. Perhaps you followed a ground rule, like not interrupting or putting anyone down. Maybe you could have probed or confronted someone, but you decided not to. Think about it for a few moments. The topic is, "A Time I Used Sharing Circle Skills Outside the Circle."

Discussion Questions:

1. What similarities and differences did you notice in the circle skills we used?
2. Why was it helpful for us to use these skills in the situations we shared?
3. How can you judge when it is appropriate to use a sharing circle skill or rule?

Life Skill Areas:

Communication, Personal Mastery, Relationships

Goals and Accomplishments

What I Would Do if I Were an Adult

Introducing the Topic:

Our Sharing Circle topic for today is, "What I Would Do if I Were an Adult." Young people are always making plans concerning what they will do when they are adults. Usually we think of the passage into adulthood as the time when we are awarded more control in our life. If you had that control right now, what would you do? Would you support your family, vote, and work to eliminate war? Would you invent something? Would you travel, own many pets, eat what and when you wish? Would you run for political office or work to save the rain forest? Think of all the things you could do if you were an adult and pick one thing to share with us. Our topic is, "What I Would Do if I Were an Adult."

Discussion Questions:

1. In your opinion, what is the best thing about being an adult?
2. What drawbacks and liabilities go with being an adult?

Life Skill Areas:

Goal Setting, Decision Making, Responsibility

Something Worth Saving For

Introducing the Topic:

Our topic for this session is, "Something Worth Saving For." If you had money and you were going to save it, for what would you save? Perhaps you are saving money now. Or maybe you successfully saved in the past. What, to you, is worth saving for? A trip? A pair of sneakers? A computer? A computer game? A baseball mitt? A bike? A jacket? A college education?

It doesn't matter how much money you save; what we want to talk about in this session is something important enough to save for and how you would do it. The topic is, "Something Worth Saving For."

Discussion Questions:

1. Why do people save?
2. What would happen if *all* people spent *all* the money they earned?
3. Why is saving money sometimes so difficult?

Life Skill Areas:

Values, Decision Making, Goal Setting

A Success I Recently Experienced

Introducing the Topic:

Our topic for today is, "A Success I Recently Experienced." If you try to do something and do it, that is a success. Have you tried to do something recently and succeeded? Maybe you decided to earn an A in a certain class and earned it. Perhaps you set out to run a mile and didn't stop until you had. Maybe you decided you didn't want to lose your temper anymore, and the next time someone made you mad, you controlled your anger. That's success! Think for a moment about some of your recent successes and share one with us. The topic is, "A Success I Recently Experienced."

Discussion Questions:

1. How did you feel when you succeeded?
2. How does one success affect your willingness to try to do something else?
3. What affect does failure have on you?
4. What does it mean to learn from a failure?

Life Skill Areas:

Self-Awareness, Goal Setting, Self-Esteem

Topic Variations:

"A Failure I Experienced Recently"
"A Time I was Successful and It Hurt Someone's Feelings"

Something I Would Like To Achieve in the Next Three Years

Introducing the Topic:

The topic for today's Sharing Circle is, "Something I Would Like To Achieve in the Next Three Years." Think for a moment about yourself right now. Then think of yourself three years from now. What would like to have, do, or be that's different from today? Maybe you'd like to become an A student, play on a sports team, learn a foreign language, study a musical instrument, form a band, start your own savings account, or write a book. You can achieve in any area you choose. Take a moment to think before you share on our topic, "Something I Would Like To Achieve in the Next Three Years."

Discussion Questions:

1. What is an achievement?
2. How do we feel about setting achievement goals?
3. How can setting goals help you direct your future?

Life Skill Areas:

Self-Awareness, Goal Setting, Responsibility

Topic Variation:

"Something I Would Like to Achieve in the Next Year"
"Something I Am Achieving Right Now"
"When I Am An Adult, I Want To..."

Something I Wish I Could Do Better

Introducing the Topic:

The topic for today is, "Something I Wish I Could Do Better." Few of us are completely satisfied with ourselves. Wanting to improve is an important step in growing and is a lifelong process. Is there something that you wish you could do better right now? Maybe you'd like to be more comfortable meeting and getting to know other people. Or perhaps you'd like to be a better ball player, or be able to draw and paint better. You might wish you were better at getting your homework done, or keeping your room clean. Think of ways in which you wish you could do better and select one you feel comfortable sharing with us. Again, the topic is, "Something I Wish I Could Do Better."

Discussion Questions:

1. How easy or difficult was it for you to share about something you would like to do better?
2. Why is it important to target areas for self-improvement?
3. How can we balance self-acceptance and the desire to improve?

Life Skill Areas:

Self-Awareness, Goal Setting

Topic Variation:

"Something About Myself I Am Proud Of"

Something I Want

Introducing the Topic:

Today our topic for discussion is, "Something I Want." We all want things. Some of us want things we must purchase, such as a bike, a car, or stereo equipment. Others of us want to achieve things, such as the ability to play a musical instrument, establish a friendship, develop an athletic skill, or become class president. Tell us about one thing that you want. Maybe you want to be an A student, or a more patient person. Perhaps you want to win a big sweepstakes, to change something about yourself, or to experience better health or greater popularity. Think about the many things you want and select one to share. The topic is, "Something I Want."

Discussion Questions:

1. How can we get the things we want?
2. How can we be sure that what we want is good for us?
3. If you have things now that you got through work and planning, how well did those things measure up to your expectations?

Life Skill Areas:

Self-Awareness, Decision Making, Goal Setting, Self-Esteem

When I Got to Share in Making a Decision

Introducing the Topic:

Today's topic is, "When I Got to Share in Making a Decision." We all like to be part of the decision-making process. We want to help our families plan vacations and decide what movies to see. We want to be involved when our friends decide how to spend Saturday afternoon. When a decision involves us, we want to express our ideas and give our input.

Tell us about a time when you helped make a group decision. You may have helped your parents decide whether or not to sign you up for dance or music lessons. Perhaps you helped make all the decisions required for a Christmas or birthday surprise. Right now, you and your parents may be deciding which college you should attend, or what color the house should be painted. It doesn't matter if the decision was big or small; we want to know how you felt and what you learned from the experience. The topic is, "When I Got to Share in Making a Decision."

Discussion Questions:

1. What are the advantages of helping to make decisions that affect you?
2. What do you usually contribute to the decision-making process?
3. How do you feel when you are a part of the decision making process?

Life Skill Areas:

Decision-Making, Self-Awareness, Personal Mastery

Something I Want, But Am Afraid to Ask For

Introducing the Topic:

Our Sharing Circle topic today is, "Something I Want, But Am Afraid to Ask For." We all want things. Some of the things we want are easy to ask for and others are more difficult. What are you afraid to ask for?

Maybe you want to be part of a group of kids at school, but are afraid to ask because you don't want to be rejected. Or maybe you want one particular person to like you, but can't quite bring yourself to make the first move. You might want to ask your parents for a new game, or stereo, or even a car. Or you might feel ready for more responsibility, later hours, or a job. If you choose to share, tell us what you want, whom you need to ask, and why you are afraid. Take a few moments to think about it. Our topic is, "Something I Want, But Am Afraid to Ask for."

Discussion Questions:

1. Why are we afraid to ask for some of the things we want?
2. What are some things we can do to overcome our fear of asking for what we want?

Life Skill Areas:

Assertiveness, Communication, Goal Setting, Self-Esteem

A Time I Won and Loved It

Introducing the Topic:

Today's topic is, "A Time I Won and Loved It." Perhaps you'll need to think about this topic a little bit, or possibly an experience you've had has already flashed into your mind.

Each of us has experienced a victorious moment, overcome a difficult situation—or done something that caused us to feel like a winner! Think of a moment like that in your life. It might have come in a game or as part of an experience in which you showed a lot of courage or accomplished something that made you feel proud afterward. Maybe you won an award or prize. Or perhaps you won someone's approval be completing a task extremely well. Take a minute to think of a time when you were the winner and felt wonderful about it. The topic is, "A Time I Won and Loved It."

Discussion Questions:

1. What similarities did you notice in the situations that caused us to feel great about winning?
2. How many of the situations we told about involved competing with others? How many involved cooperating with others?
3. What are some differences between competing and cooperating?

Life Skill Areas:

Goal Setting, Personal Mastery, Self-Awareness

A Time I Lost and Took It Hard

Introducing the Topic:

Our topic for this session is, "A Time I Lost and Took It Hard." You may have to think about this one a little bit. The idea is to remember a time when you wanted very much to win at something, and worked at it and put all your hopes into it, so when you lost you felt really bad.

Maybe you tried out for something and thought you had it made or hoped very much that you would be chosen. Perhaps you studied hard for a test, and thought you had all the answers. Maybe you were trying to win a prize, but somebody else won it instead. This may be something that happened to you recently, or it could have occurred a long time ago. Take a minute to think about it. The topic is, "A Time I Lost and Took It Hard."

Discussion Questions:

1. What makes certain losses particularly difficult to take?
2. Do you think winning ever becomes too important to people? When?
3. Do there always have to be losers in order to have winners, or can you think of situations in which everybody can win?

Life Skill Areas:

Self-Awareness, Values

First I Imagined It, and Then I Created It

Introducing the Topic:

The topic for our session today is, "First I Imagined It, and Then I Created It." Have you ever created something after thinking about it for awhile first? Perhaps you created a drawing in your mind before putting it on paper, or developed a story in your imagination before writing it down. Maybe you arranged your room first by envisioning how it would look, or planned a dinner menu in your mind before starting to prepare it. The imagining may have taken the form of slow, careful planning, it may have occurred in a flash of inspiration, or perhaps the idea came to you in a dream. Give it some thought. The topic is, "First I Imagined it, and Then I Created It."

Discussion Questions:

1. What similarities did you notice in the ways our imagination helped us create? What differences did you notice?
2. What role does imagination play when you are creating or inventing?
3. Everyone gets good ideas from time to time. In order to be creative, what do people need to do with their ideas?

Life Skill Areas:

Goal Setting, Personal Mastery, Creativity

When Someone Expected the Very Best of Me

Introducing the Topic:

Our session for today is about expectations. The topic is, "When Someone Expected the Very Best of Me." Can you think of a time when you were expected to do your best on a task or project?

Maybe you were involved in an athletic event, a game, or some kind of school project, and a parent or teacher let you know that you were capable of an outstanding performance. Or maybe you were about to try out for a part in a play and a friend encouraged you be saying, "You'll do great!" The important thing to consider is how you were affected by the person who expected the very best from you. Perhaps you felt bolstered by this person's faith in you, or maybe the pressure was uncomfortable. Maybe you felt both ways at the same time. Take a minute to think of a time like this and tell us about what happened and how you felt. The topic is, "When Someone Expected the Very Best of Me."

Discussion Questions:

1. How did most of us perform when someone expected us to do well?
2. When someone expects a person to do poorly, what generally happens? Why?
3. What have you learned about how people influence each other from this session?

Life Skill Areas:

Self-Awareness, Goal Setting, Personal Mastery, Relationships

Things I Can Do To Get Where I Want To Be

Introducing The Topic:

Today's topic is, "Things I Can Do to Get Where I Want To Be." The theme of this topic is very important to consider when you want to achieve something. To reach any kind of a goal, it is very important to think of all the steps you will have to take. This is true whether your goal is immediate, like getting a good grade on a test, or long term, like wanting to travel to a foreign country when you get out of school. Whatever it is, you need to be aware of all the things it takes to get what you want.

Think of one of your goals. Now try to picture yourself doing everything necessary to reach that goal. Do you have to learn a new skill or language? Do you have to read books or talk with people in order to get information? Will you have to change your way of thinking, or strengthen your body, or move to another city? This is a complex topic, so take your time. When you're ready to share, the topic is, "Things I Can Do to Get Where I Want To Be."

Discussion Questions:

1. Why is it important to be aware of what it takes to reach a goal?
2. Although we all shared about different goals, what similarities did you notice in the steps it will take to reach them? What differences did you notice?

Life Skill Areas:

Goal Setting, Self-Awareness, Personal Mastery

What I Could Do To Be a Good Parent

Introducing the Topic:

Our topic for today's sharing circle is, "What I Could Do To Be a Good Parent." You probably know quite a few people who are parents. In addition, you've seen a lot of parents and a lot of people practicing parenthood. You may occasionally have reacted to things you've seen, both positively and negatively. You've also spent many hours involved in various family situations, so you know something about what goes on in families.

Suppose for a moment that you have children someday. What positive things could you do with and for your children? Could you read to them? ...play with them? ...teach them certain values? ...discipline them? What are some of the most important things you can think of? Take a few moments to consider, "What I Could Do To Be a Good Parent."

Discussion Questions:

1. What ideas did you hear in this session that you had never thought about before?
2. What similarities did you notice in the kinds of things we believe are important?
3. How do people learn to be good parents?

Life Skill Areas:

Relationships, Self-Awareness, Responsibility, Goal Setting

How I Earned Something and What I Did With It

Introducing the Topic:

Today let's talk about, "How I Earned Something and What I Did With It." Think about a time when you did some kind of work and earned something for it. It doesn't necessarily have to be money that you earned. Maybe you earned a special dinner, or a day off from your chores, or someone's respect.

Tell us what you did and how you did it and, if you want to, tell us what you earned. Was doing this job your idea, or did someone else ask you to do it? Finally, remember to tell us how you used what you earned. If you earned money, did you save it or buy something with it? If you earned something other than money, what became of it? Give it some thought. The topic is, "How I Earned Something and What I Did With It."

Discussion Questions:

1. What new ideas did you get from this circle about ways to earn money? ...to spend money?
2. What new ideas did you get about things you can earn other than money?
3. How does work help us get the things we want? How is work created?

Life Skill Areas:

Self-Awareness, Decision Making, Goal Setting, Responsibility

I Had a Problem and Solved It

Introducing the Topic:

Today's circle focuses on something you did in the past, so take a moment to think back. The topic is, "I Had A Problem and Solved It." Problems are something we all have throughout life. It's not possible to live without problems, but it is possible to solve them.

Think of a problem that you experienced some time in your past and solved. Maybe it had to do with a class or requirement at school. Perhaps the problem was associated with a close friendship, or was centered around your home life. If you choose to share, describe the problem, how you solved it, and the feelings you had when you managed it successfully. Our topic is, "I Had a Problem and Solved It."

Discussion Questions:

1. What did you learn from this session about problems?
2. What are some problem-solving strategies that you heard mentioned today?

Life Skill Areas:

Problem Solving, Awareness, Personal Mastery

Topic Variations:

Numerous topics can be created to help students develop awareness and skills in the area of problem solving. Several that we recommend are:

"A Problem That Wouldn't Go Away Until I Faced It"
"I Had a Problem, But It Didn't Get Me Down"
"When The Easy Way Out Of a Problem Made Things Worse"

Where to Find More Sharing Circles

The following products from Innerchoice Publishing include a wide variety of Sharing Circle topics:

Elementary

THE BEST SELF-ESTEEM ACTIVITIES
for the Elementary Grades

CREATING SUCCESS!
A Program for Behaviorally and Academically At-Risk Children

CLASSROOM CONNECTIONS
A Sourcebook for Teaching Stress Management and Fostering Self-Esteem

TEACHING THE SKILLS OF CONFLICT RESOLUTION
Activities and Strategies for Counselors and Teachers

INSIGHTS
A Self and Career Awareness Program for the Elementary Grades

Secondary

IMPACT!
A Self-Esteem Based Skill-Development Program for Secondary Students

Drug Prevention

JUST SAY I KNOW HOW
Drug, Alcohol and Tobacco Prevention Program for the Elementary Grades

PRIME TIME
A Comprehensive Drug Education Program
Level I   Grades K-3
Level II   Grades 4-6
Level III   Middle School
Level IV   High School

Families

FAMILY CONNECTIONS
Teaching Your Children the Skills of Self-Esteem and Drug Prevention

Poster

Sharing Circle Rules
A colorful way to help your students remember the rules

Jalmar Press and Innerchoice Publishing are happy to announce

a collaborative effort under which all Innerchoice titles will now be distributed

only through Jalmar Press.

To request the latest catalog of our joint resources for use by teachers, counselors

and other care-givers to empower children to develop inner-directed living and

learning skills

call us at: (800) 662-9662

or fax us at: (310) 816-3092

or send us a card at: P.O. Box 1185, Torrance, CA 90505

We're eager to serve you and the students you work with.

By the way, Jalmar Press / Innerchoice Publishing have a new series coming up
that can give you all the necessary tools to teach emotional intelligence to all your
students, grades K - 12.

Three titles will be available in fall, 1998.
Write or call for the latest information or to place your order.

Talking With Kids: Guided Discussions for Developing Emotional Intelligence

Guided discussions are the EQ super-strategy and this book is chock full of them! What better way to develop the emotional intelligence of your students than by participation in relevant discussions about things that are important to them. This powerful and versatile instructional strategy is unusually effective as a tool for developing —

- **self-awareness**
- **self-control**
- **the ability to understand and manage feelings**
- **empathy**
- **cooperation**
- **responsibility**
- **communication**
- **strategies for managing conflict and stress, and**
- **group interaction skills**

Included in this book:

- 89 fully developed guided discussion topics
- Suggestions for introducing each topic to students
- Key questions to ask to facilitate higher level thinking, discovery, and insight
- A comprehensive introduction to Emotional Intelligence
- Step-by-step instructions for leading Guided Discussions
- Suggestions for organizing Guided Discussions and managing the rest of the class
- Guidelines for developing your own Guided Discussion topics

INNERCHOICE PUBLISHING
P.O. BOX 1185 • TORRANCE, CA 90505
Tel. (310) 816-3085 Fax (310) 816-3092